Victorian City and Country Houses

Plans and Details

Geo. E. Woodward

DOVER PUBLICATIONS, INC.
Mineola, New York

Bibliographical Note

This Dover edition, first published in 1996, is an unabridged republication of the work first published by The American News Company, New York, in 1877 under the title *Woodward's National Architect. / Vol. II. / Containing Original Designs, Plans and Details, / To Working Scale, for / City and Country Houses.*

Library of Congress Cataloging-in-Publication Data

Woodward, George E. (George Evertson), 1829–1905.
   [Woodward's national architect. Volume II]
   Victorian city and country houses : plans and designs / Geo. E. Woodward.
      p.   cm.
   Originally published: Woodward's national architect. Volume II. New York : The American News Co., 1877.
   Includes index.
   ISBN-13: 978-0-486-29080-5
   ISBN-10: 0-486-29080-8
   1. Architecture, Domestic—United States—Designs and plans.
I. Title.
NA7205.W66 1996
728′.022′1—dc20
                                            95-43860
                                              CIP

Printed in Canada
29080806   2025
www.doverpublications.com

DESCRIPTION OF PLATES ALL DRAWN TO WORKING SCALE.

CONTENTS.

DESIGN A.

PLATES ONE TO EIGHT.

FIVE HOUSES ON ONE CITY LOT. 25 x 100 FEET.

In presenting this design in the shape it is, several objects are accomplished.

The front elevation is an elevation not only for five houses having a depth of twenty-five feet, but for five houses having any depth required, and any plan of the same width may be adapted to each of the five houses in the elevation.

The elevation also may be adapted to a variety of purposes by changes in the basement story, and be made useful as a public building, library, hall, school, or hotel, being then treated as one entire building.

This design, therefore, in the hands of an ingenious architect or builder, supplies the suggestions for a large number of distinct buildings, giving one single house twenty feet front; two houses, three houses, four houses, five houses, and one entire building for any purpose.

This design for five independent small houses, to be built on one corner lot 25 x 100 feet, has frequently been carried out of late years in New York, and has accommodated a class unable to rent large houses, and unwilling to adopt the tenement and New York "flat systems." The independent house will always command owners or tenants not familiar with the "apartment" system, and the great objection to the arbitrary size of a New York City lot is that, without great loss, it cannot be made available in the construction of houses of moderate capacity.

PLATE 1.

DESIGN. A.

STREET ELÉVATION

SCALE

0 1 2 3 4 5 6 7 8 9 10   15   20   25

SECTION.   AVENUE ELEVATION.

SCALE

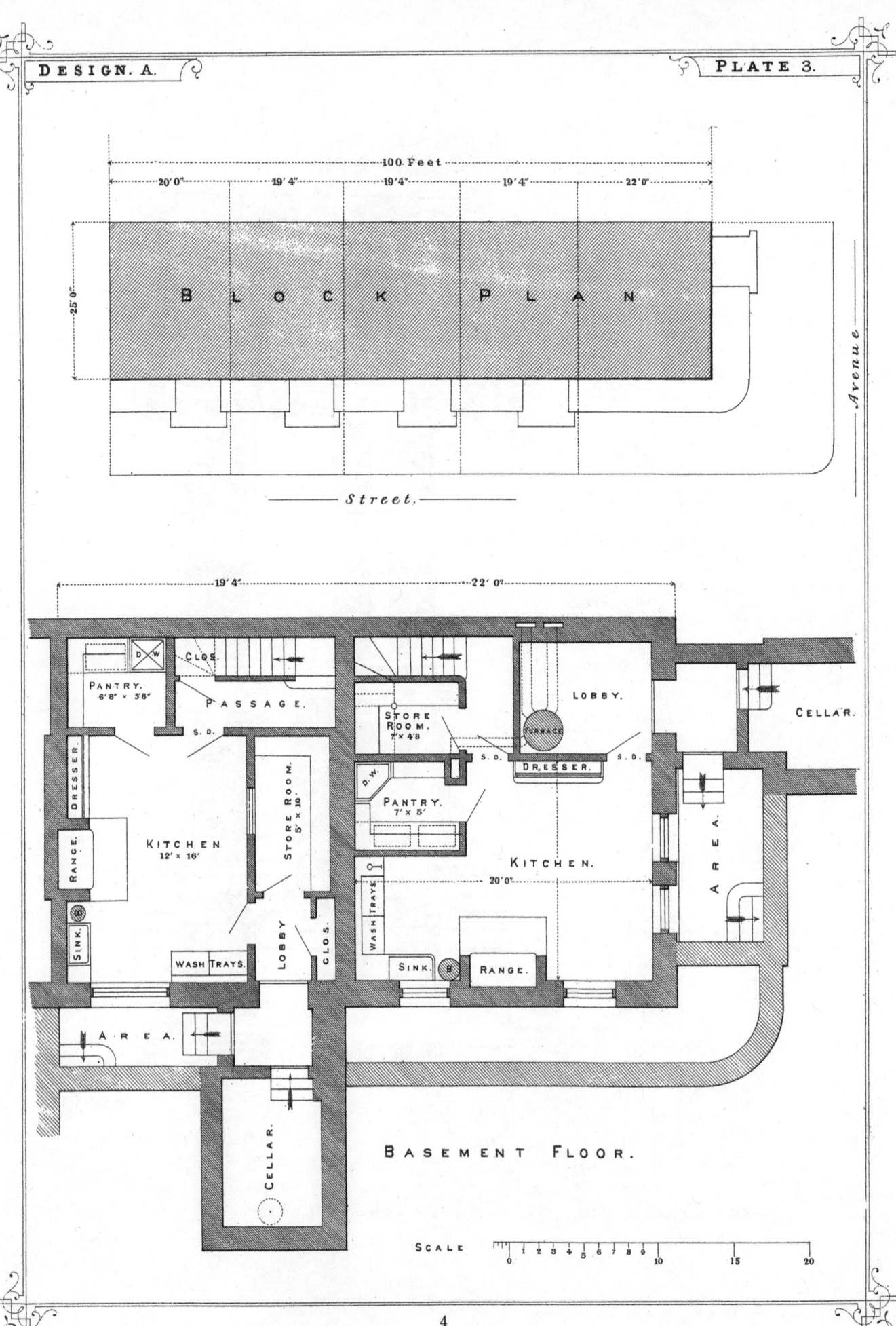

100 Feet

20' 0"   19' 4"   19' 4"   19' 4"   22' 0"

25' 0"

B L O C K   P L A N

Avenue

Street.

19' 4"   22' 0"

PANTRY.
6'8" × 5'8"

CLOS.

PASSAGE.

STORE ROOM.
7'× 4'8

LOBBY.

FURNACE

CELLAR.

DRESSER.

S.D.

DRESSER.

S.D.

S.D.

D.W

PANTRY.
7'× 5'

RANGE.

KITCHEN
12' × 16'

STORE ROOM.
5' × 10'

O.W.

KITCHEN.

20'0"

AREA.

SINK.

WASH TRAYS.

WASH TRAYS.

LOBBY

CLOS.

SINK.

RANGE.

AREA.

AREA.

CELLAR.

BASEMENT FLOOR.

SCALE   0 1 2 3 4 5 6 7 8 9 10   15   20

ENGLISH BASEMENT.

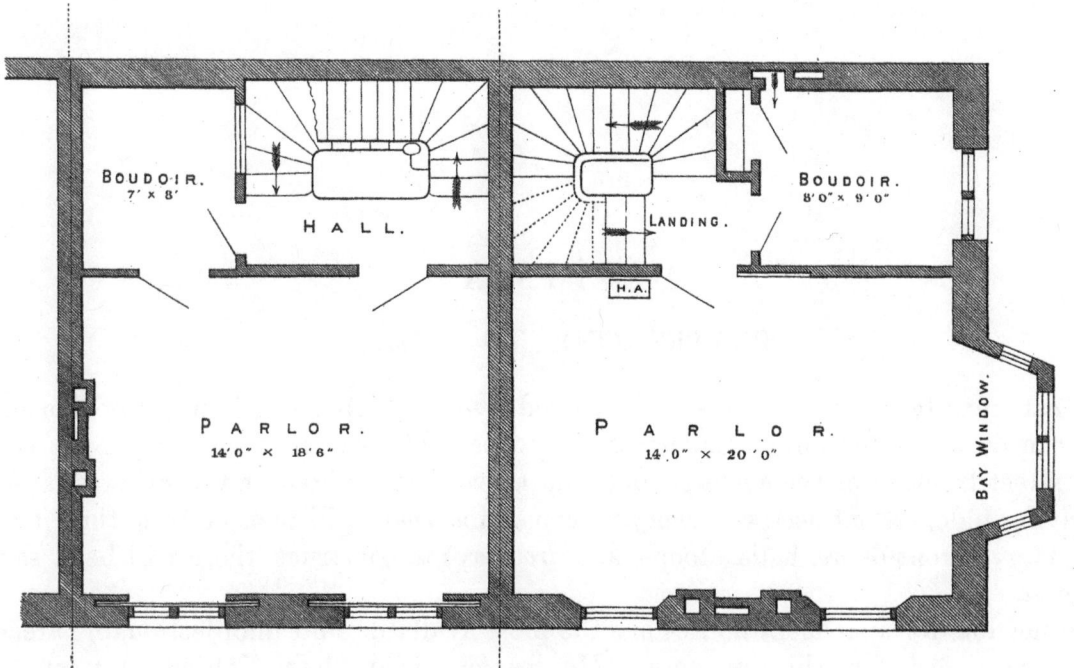

PARLOR FLOOR.

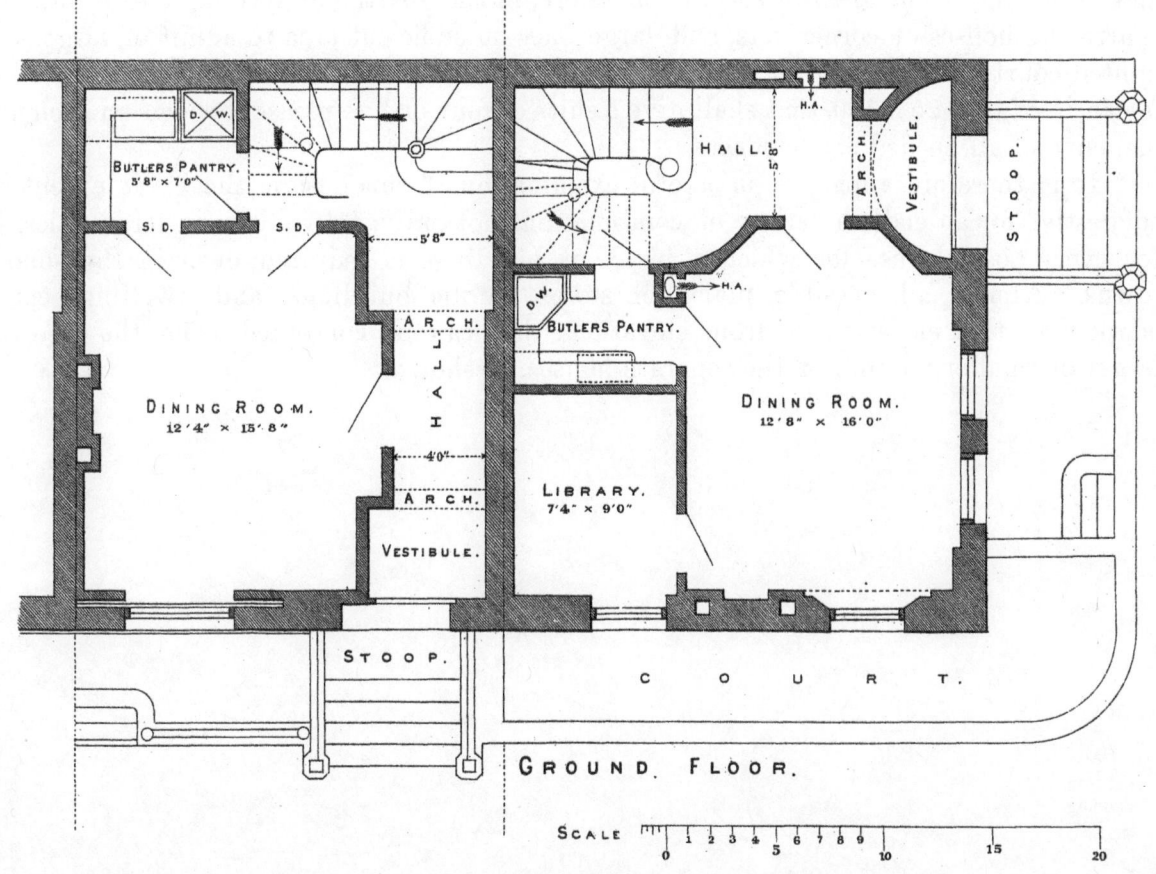

GROUND FLOOR.

SCALE

0 1 2 3 4 5 6 7 8 9 10 15 20

DESIGN A.

PLATES ONE TO EIGHT.

It can readily be seen by one with a good eye for adaptation, how easily this entire design can be converted for an "apartment" house. The entrance may be in the center of the street front, or at the avenue front, and a rear hall lighted and ventilated at both ends, giving independent access to every room; and as there will then be from three to four less stairways, front doors, halls, stoops, and areaways to construct, there will be a saving in the cost.

Corner lots for apartment houses are the most available and unobjectionable areas of 2,500 square feet for this purpose. Houses on inside lots, lighted only at front and rear, not only do not occupy the full lot, but all the inside rooms are usually dark and uncomfortable. The greatest success, therefore, in the apartment system, is to build small apartment houses on corner lots, and large ones on sufficient area to admit of large, well-lighted courts. It is, however, possible by the use of a court, to plan a house of this kind for an inside lot 25 x 100, that shall give a suite of four or five pleasant rooms on each floor, inclusive of all needed conveniences.

It is therefore apparent, on careful examination of this design, the great extent it is suggestive for an endless variety of combinations not only as dwellings in large cities, but for every possible use for which a block of buildings is required, even in the smallest towns. Almost all possible plans for stores, public buildings, and dwellings can be adapted to this elevation, or from elevations that can be combined from the use of a larger or smaller number of the separate houses, as shown.

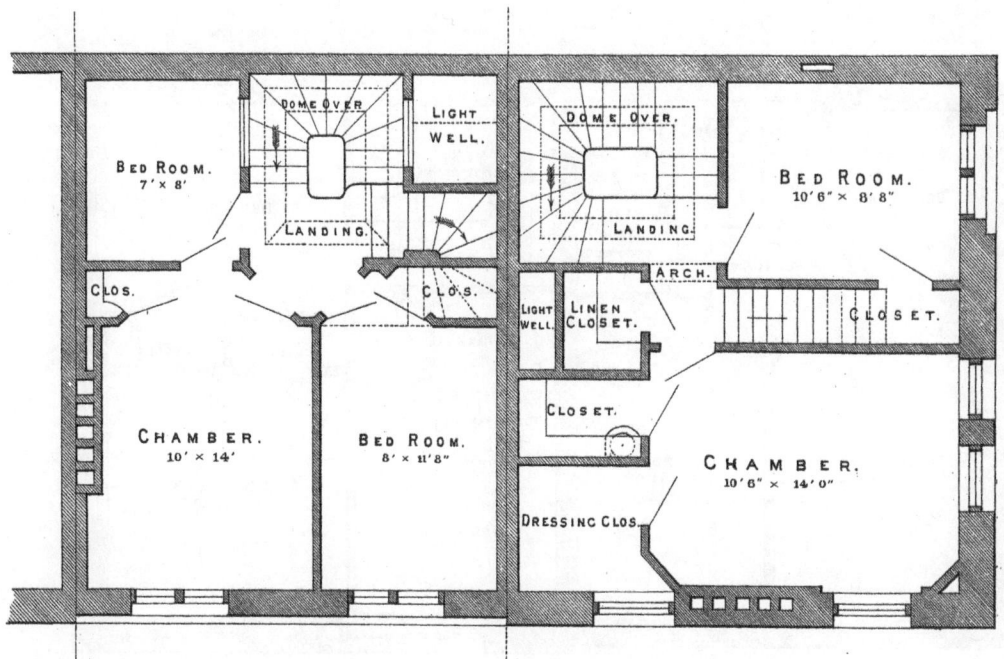

2D. CHAMBER FLOOR.

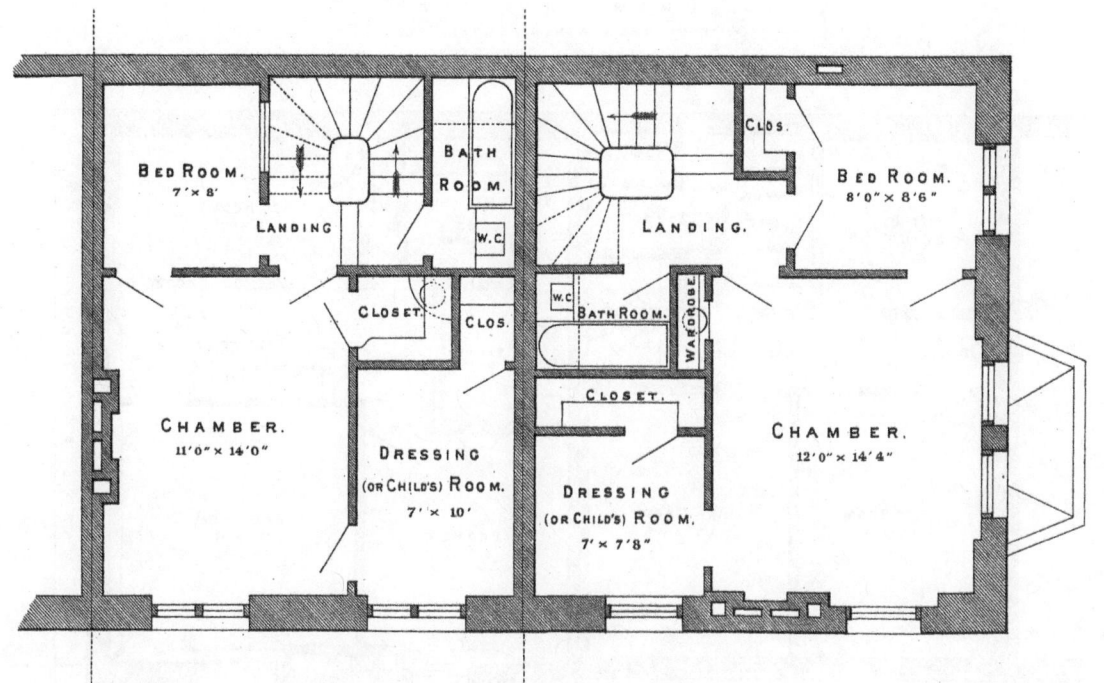

1ST. CHAMBER FLOOR.

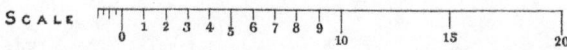

SCALE 0 1 2 3 4 5 6 7 8 9 10 15 20

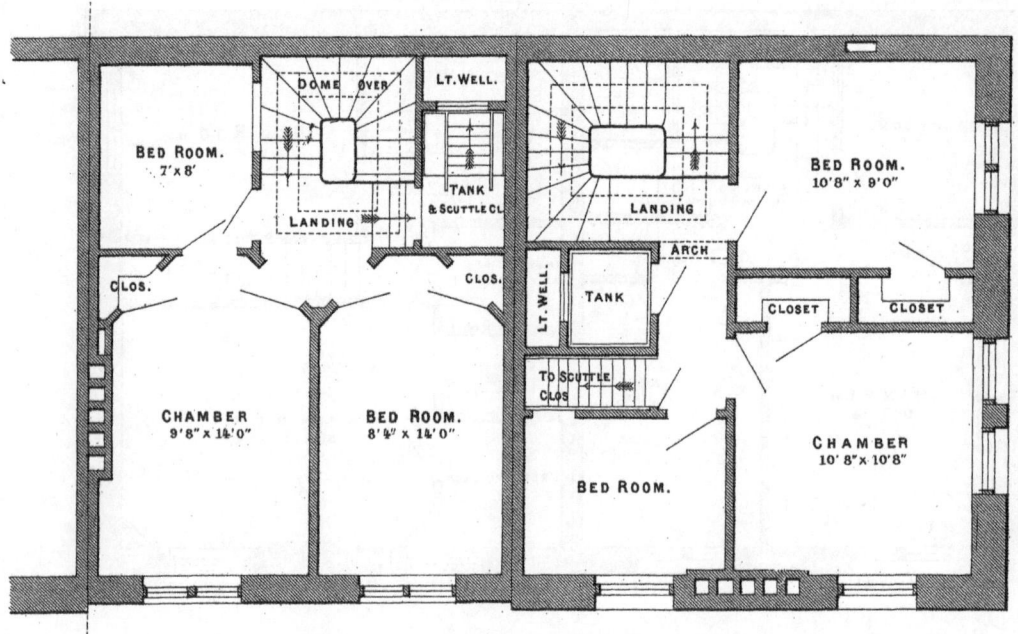

2D. CHAMBER FLOOR
(WITHOUT THE FRENCH ROOF)

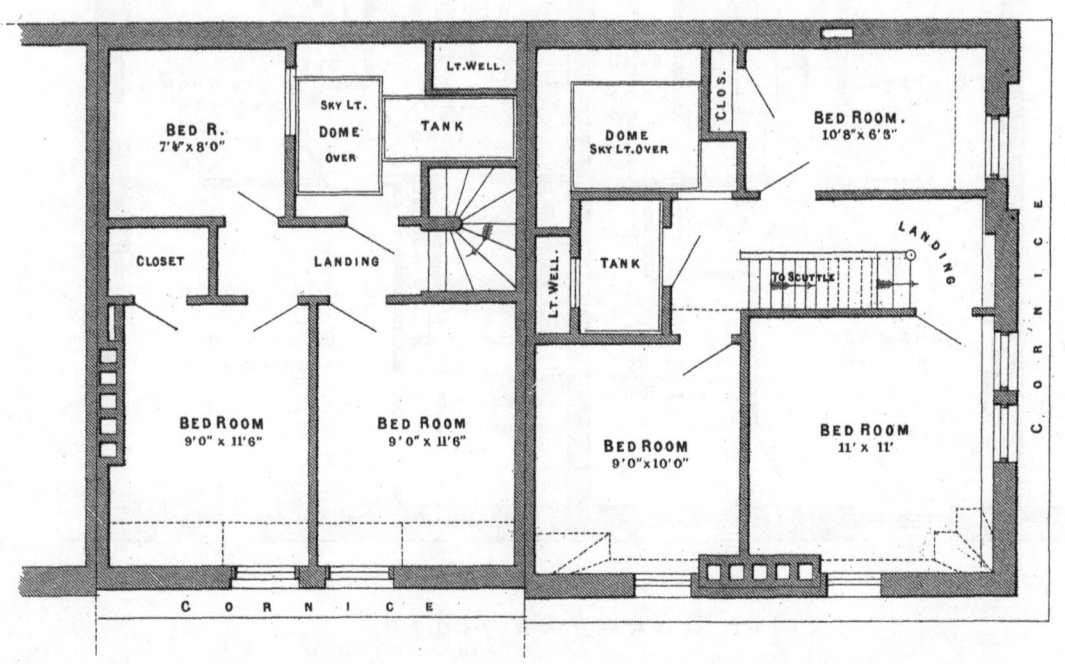

ATTIC FLOOR

SCALE

PLATE 7.

SCALE 12 9 6 3 0 1 2 3 4 5 Feet

D

B   A

ENLARGED AT ℥ LEADER B

ENLARGED AT "A"

ENLARGED AT "C"

ENLARGED AT "D"

CAP OF LARGER DORMER

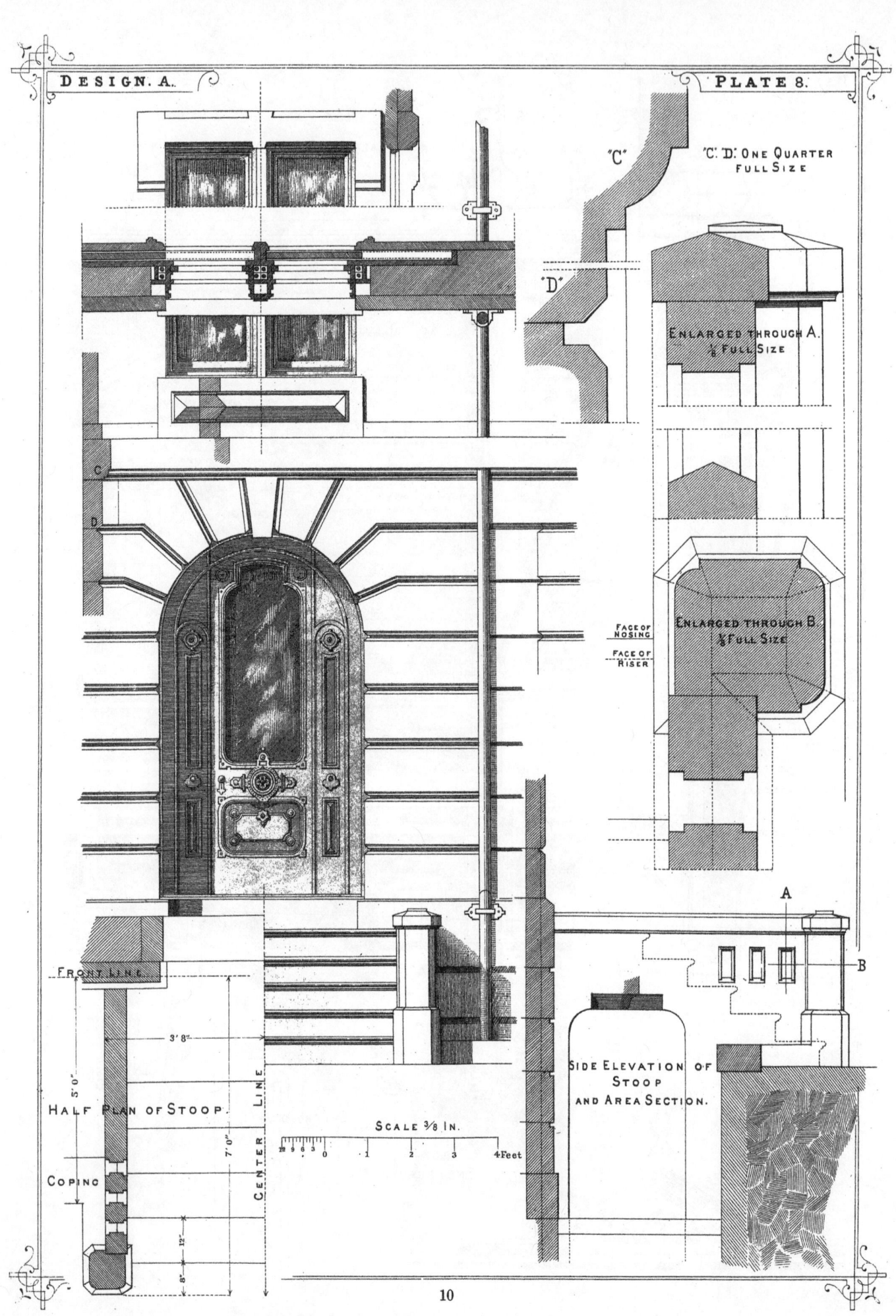

"C"

"C" "D" ONE QUARTER
FULL SIZE

"D"

ENLARGED THROUGH A.
⅛ FULL SIZE

FACE OF
NOSING

FACE OF
RISER

ENLARGED THROUGH B.
⅛ FULL SIZE

C

D

A

B

FRONT LINE.

3' 8"

5' 0"

HALF PLAN OF STOOP.

CENTER LINE

7' 0"

SIDE ELEVATION OF
STOOP
AND AREA SECTION.

COPING

12"

8"

SCALE ⅜ IN.

12 9 6 3 0   1   2   3   4 Feet

DESIGN B.

PLATES 9, 10, 11, 12 & 13.

This design, with a French or mansard roof, is well adapted for erection in wood, brick or stone, and is a very attractive as well as a convenient house, and one that can be readily changed to suit any site or exposure. Drawings to scale of sixteen feet to an inch.

House built in wood, will cost about $6,000.

DESIGN C.

PLATES 14, 15 & 16.

For a convenient house of moderate cost this arrangement of rooms and style of architecture will be found well adapted, the first story to have a ceiling of 10 feet, and the second story nine feet. The plan is carefully figured, and all the drawings are to a scale of one-sixteenth of an inch to one foot.

House built in wood will cost about $3,000.

FRONT ELEVATION

SIDE ELEVATION.

SCALE. 1/16 Inch to One Foot.

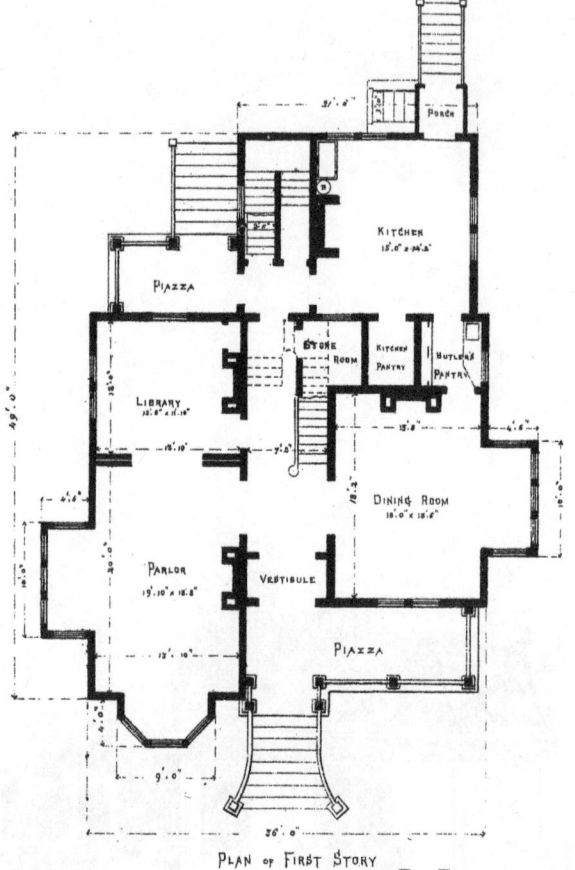

PLAN OF FIRST STORY

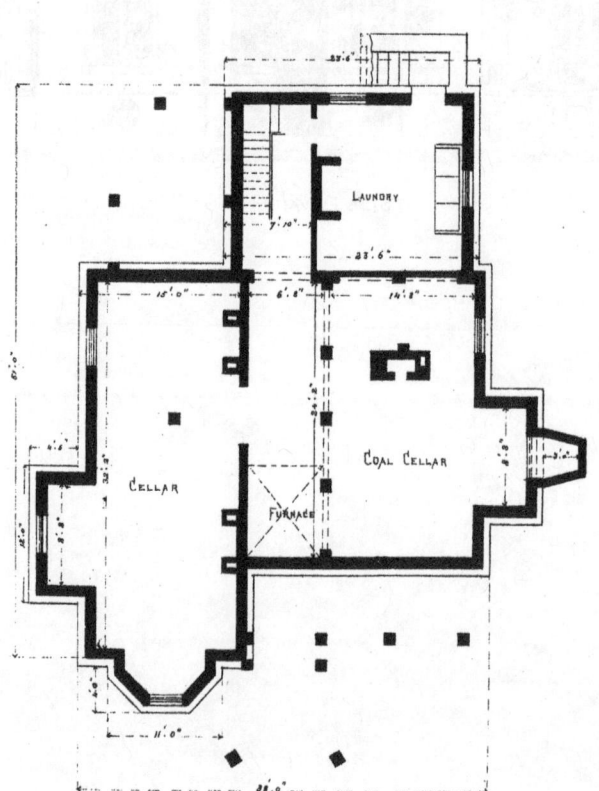

SCALE ½ INCH TO THE FOOT   PLAN OF BASEMENT

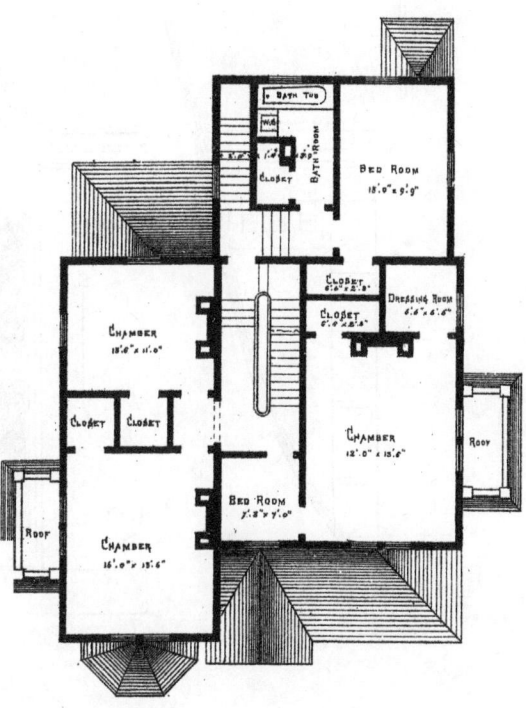

PLAN OF SECOND STORY

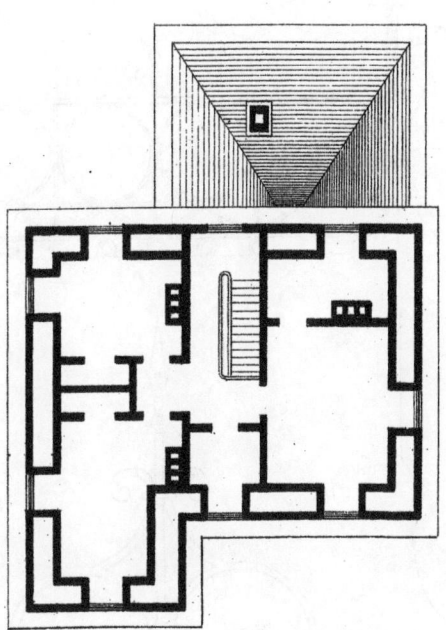

PLAN OF ATTIC

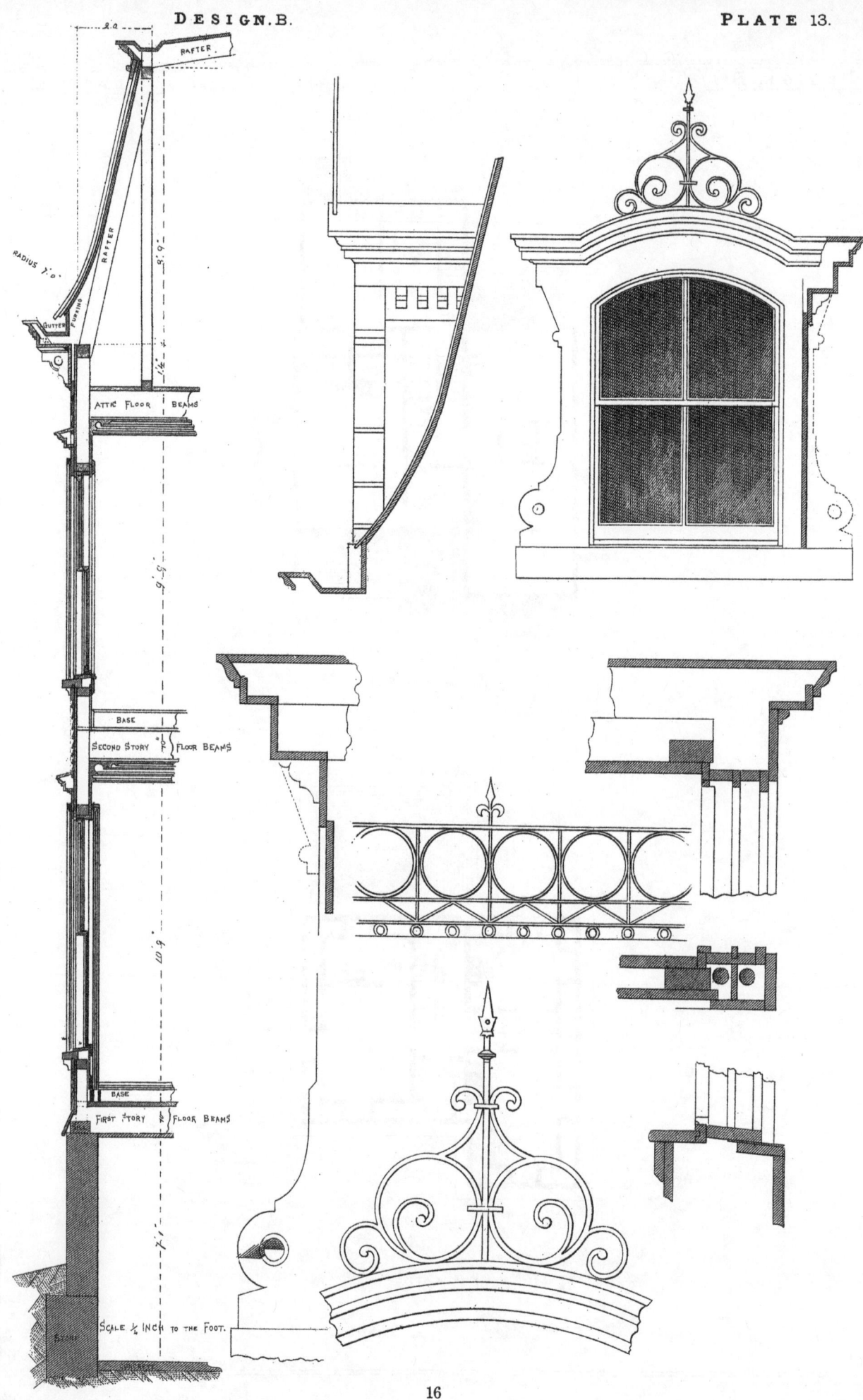

SCALE ½ INCH TO THE FOOT.

FRONT ELEVATION

SIDE ELEVATION.

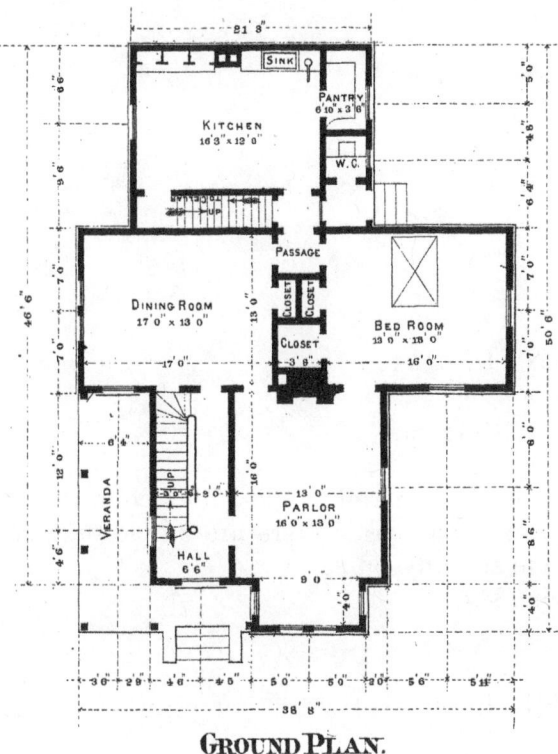

GROUND PLAN.

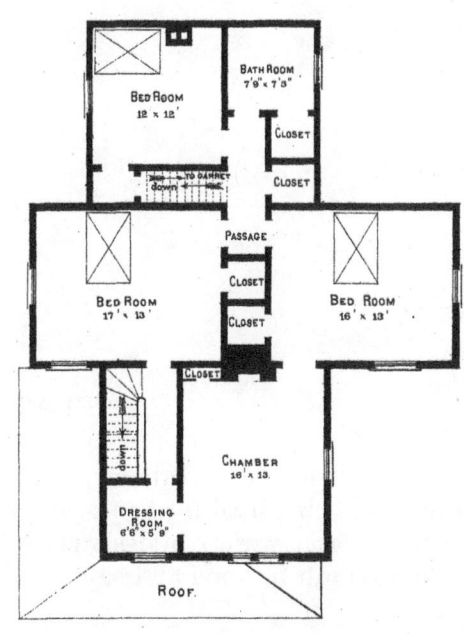

CHAMBER PLAN.

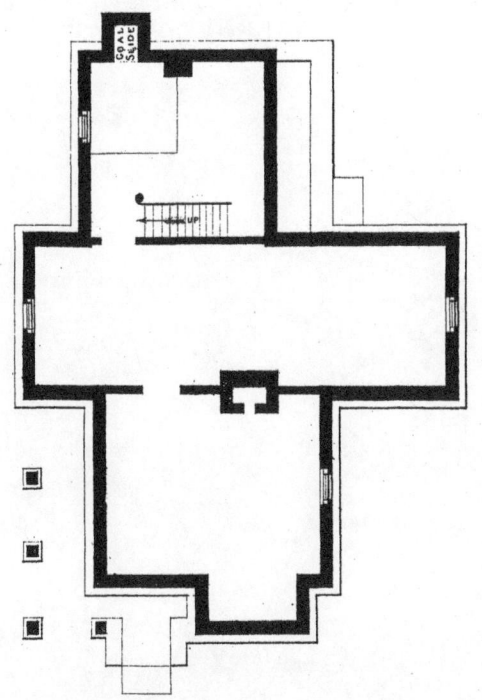

CELLAR PLAN.

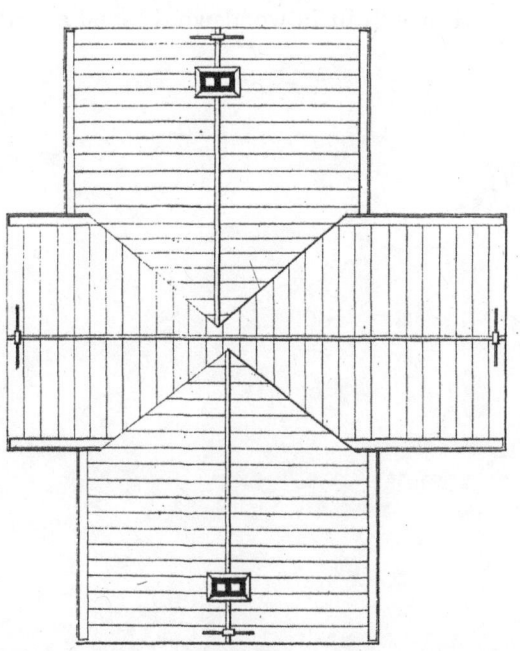

ROOF PLAN.

DESIGN D.

PLATES 17, 18, 19 & 20.

This design is in the ornamental German style, which is well adapted for a country house, and admits of being used for houses of almost every size and cost. Here are ample suggestions from which a large variety of designs can be made to suit any purse.

House built in wood and stone will cost about $8,500.

DESIGN E.

PLATES 21, 22, 23 & 24.

Here is a design for a village or suburban house, of a very attractive exterior and with two differently arranged sets of plans. This house would look well in almost any locality. The drawings are to a scale of sixteen feet to an inch.

House built in wood would cost about $4,500.

FRONT ELEVATION

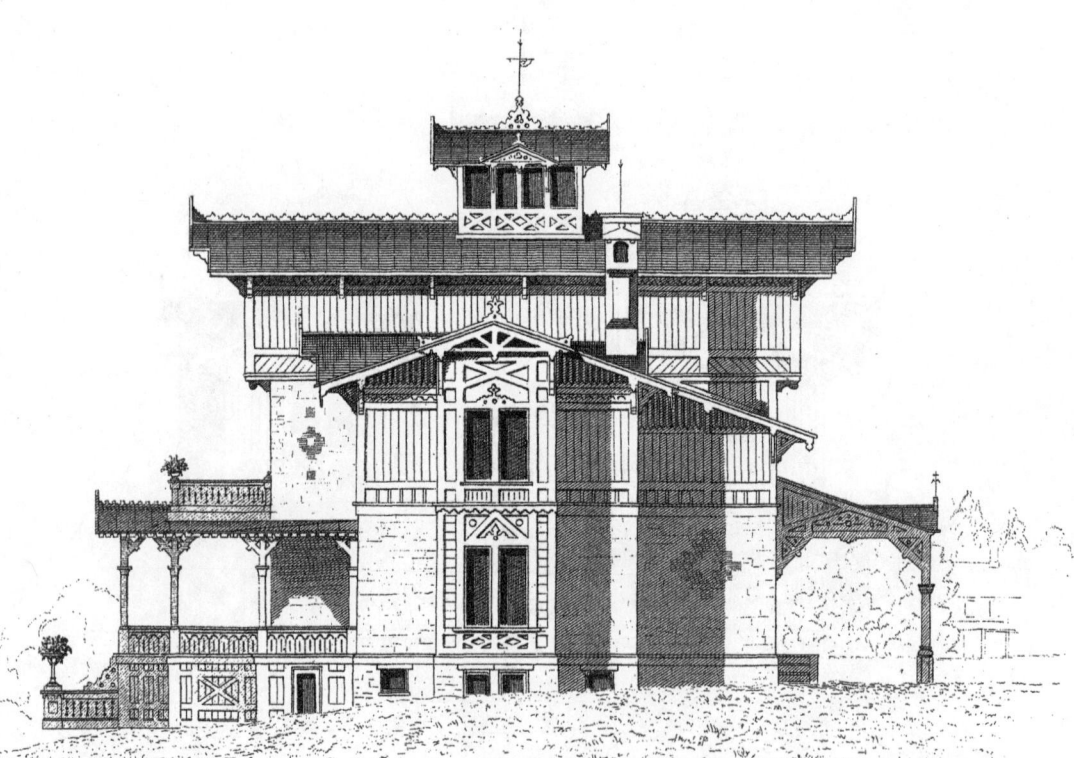

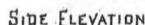

SIDE ELEVATION.

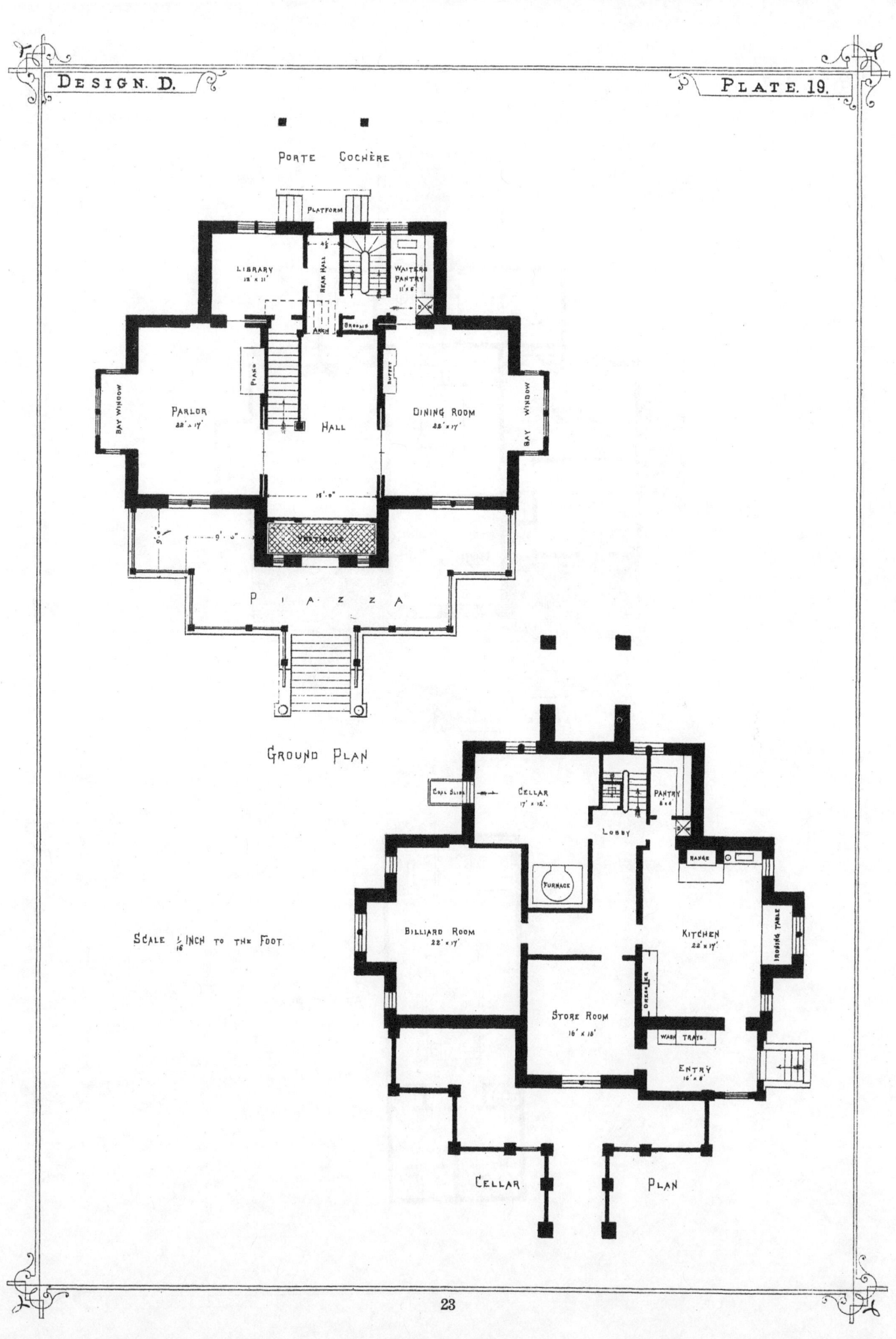

PORTE COCHÈRE

PLATFORM

LIBRARY
13' x 11'

REAR HALL

WAITERS
PANTRY
11' x 8'

BROOMS

ARCH

PIANO

BAY WINDOW

PARLOR
22' x 17'

HALL

BUFFET

DINING ROOM
22' x 17'

BAY WINDOW

15'0"

9' 0"

VESTIBULE

P I A Z Z A

GROUND PLAN

SCALE ½/16 INCH TO THE FOOT

COAL SLIDE

CELLAR
17' x 12'

PANTRY
8' x 6'

LOBBY

FURNACE

RANGE

BILLIARD ROOM
22' x 17'

DRESSER

STORE ROOM
16' x 15'

KITCHEN
22' x 17'

IRONING TABLE

WASH TRAYS

ENTRY
16' x 8'

CELLAR   PLAN

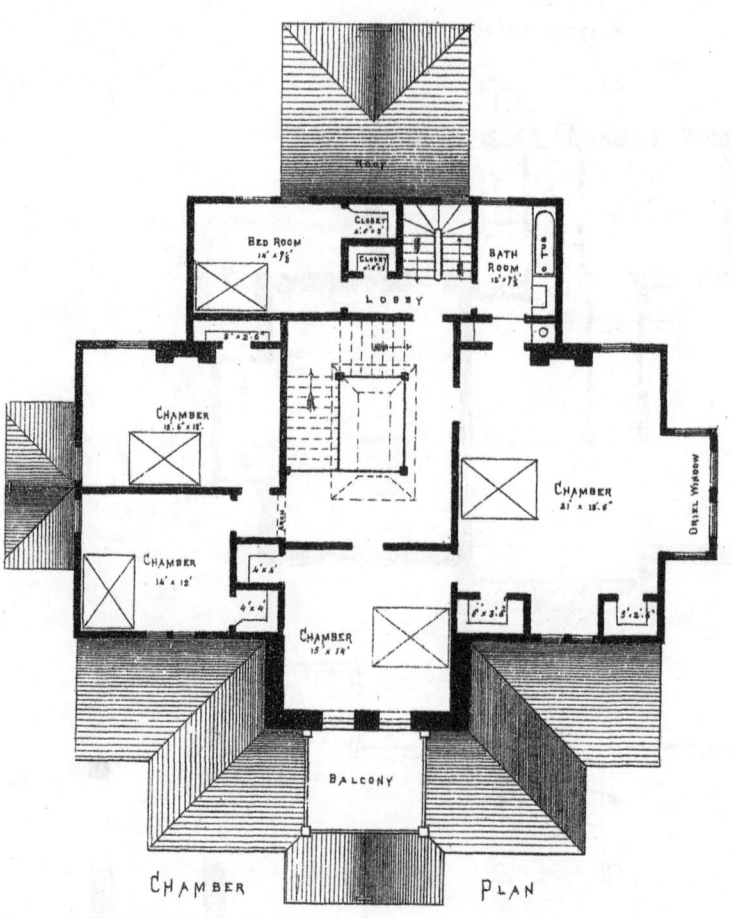

CHAMBER　　　　PLAN

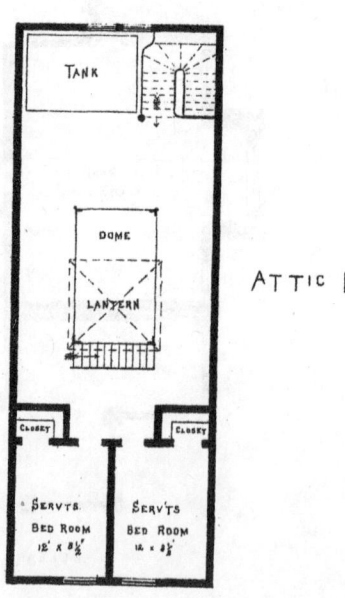

ATTIC PLAN

FRONT ELEVATION

SIDE ELEVATION.

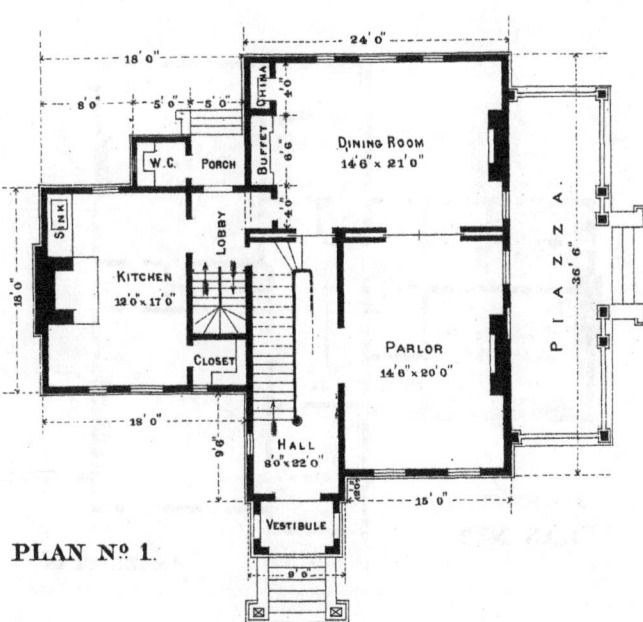

PLAN Nº 1.

GROUND PLAN.

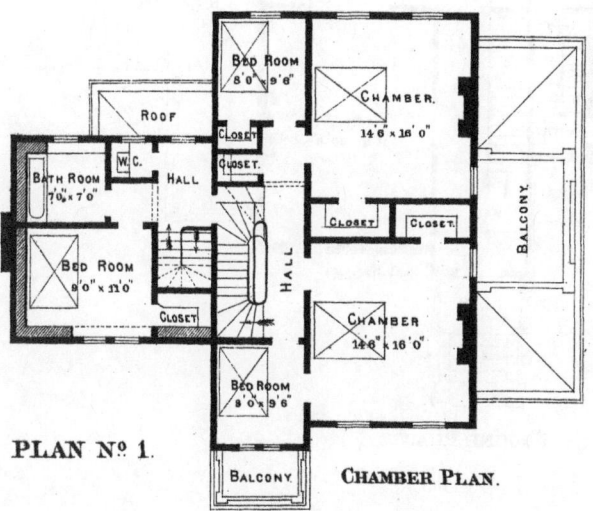

PLAN Nº 1.   CHAMBER PLAN.

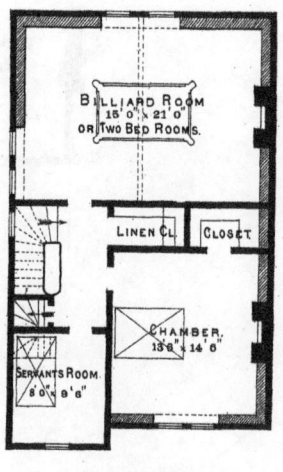

ATTIC PLAN.

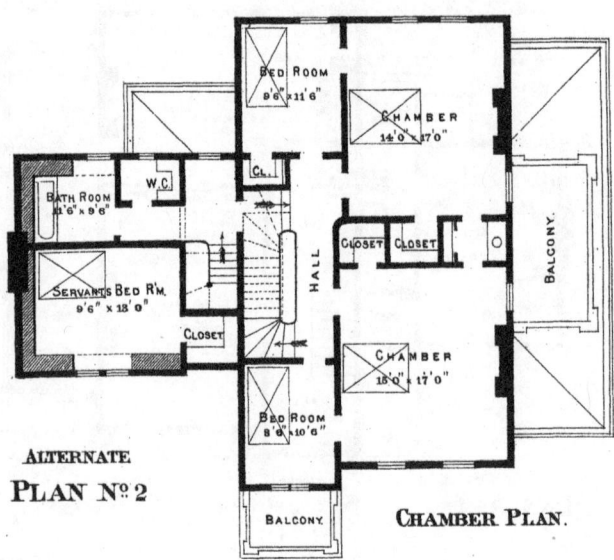

ALTERNATE
PLAN N° 2

CHAMBER PLAN.

ALTERNATE
PLAN N° 2

(WITH KITCHEN IN BASEMENT.)

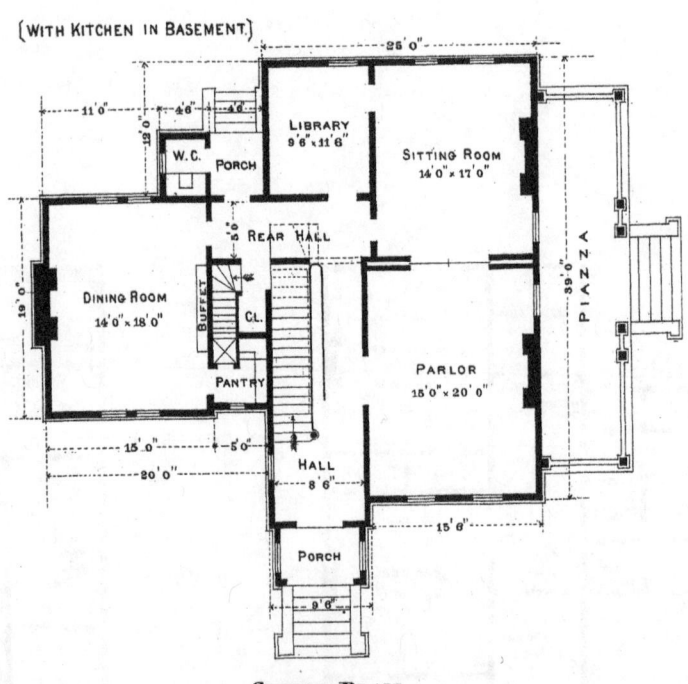

GROUND PLAN.

DESIGN F.

PLATES 25, 26, 27 & 28.

This design presents a great variety, especially in the several arrangements of the different groups of windows, which, in arranging another design of similar character, will be found of considerable service.   Drawings to a scale of sixteen feet to an inch.

House will cost about $5,500.

DESIGN G.

PLATES 29, 30, 31 & 32.

For a roomy, low priced house, this design will be found very useful.   The piazza, bay window and rear extension give a variety to the exterior, while the interior has a convenient arrangement and independent access to all rooms.   Drawings to scale of sixteen feet to an inch.

House will cost about $3,000.

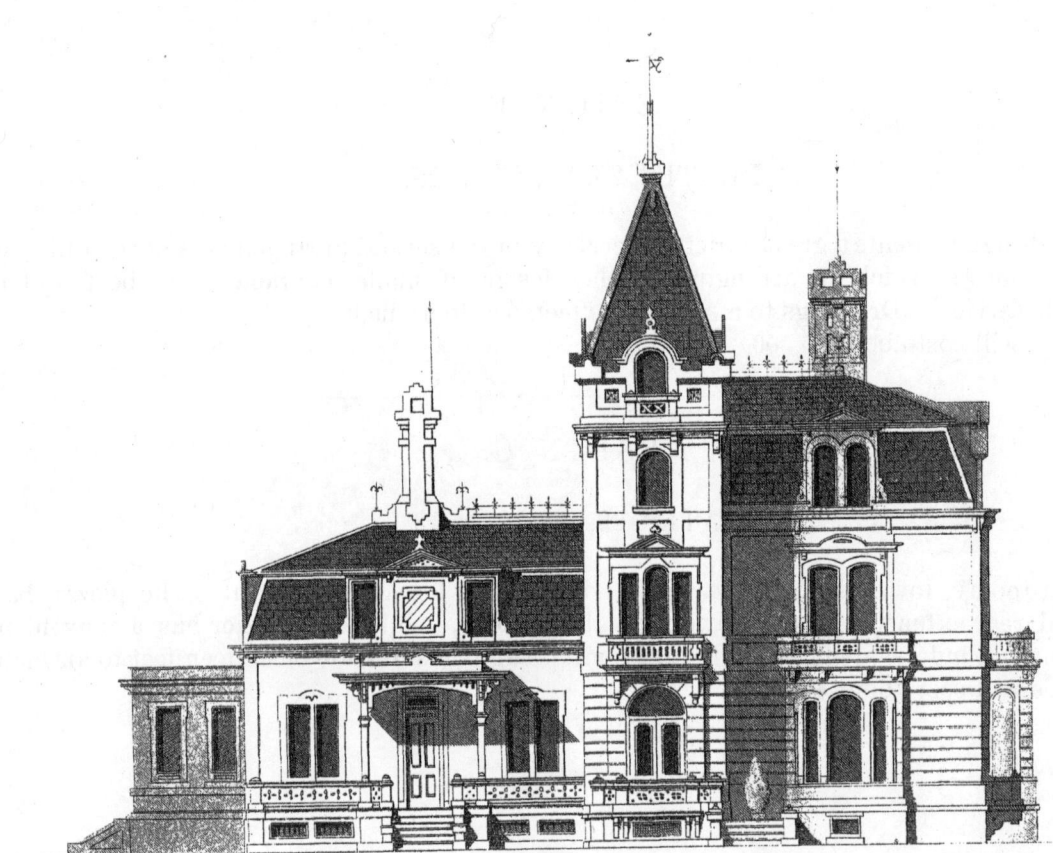

FRONT ELEVATION

SIDE ELEVATION.

SCALE. 1/16 Inch to One Foot.

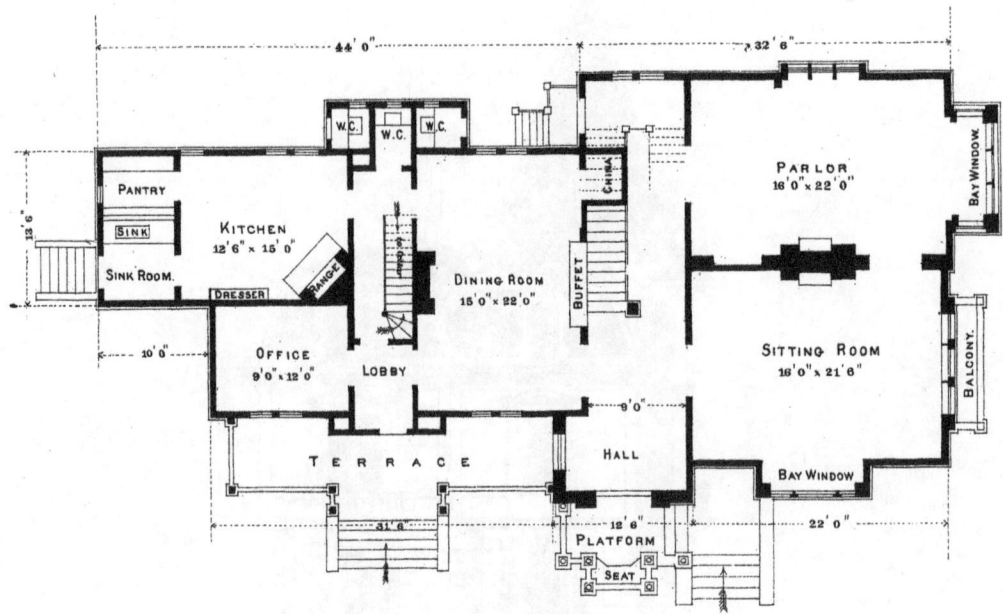

GROUND PLAN

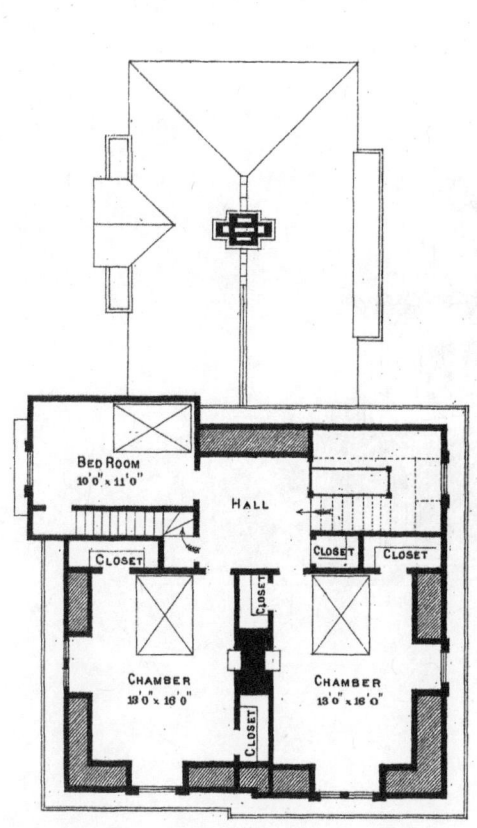

ATTIC PLAN.

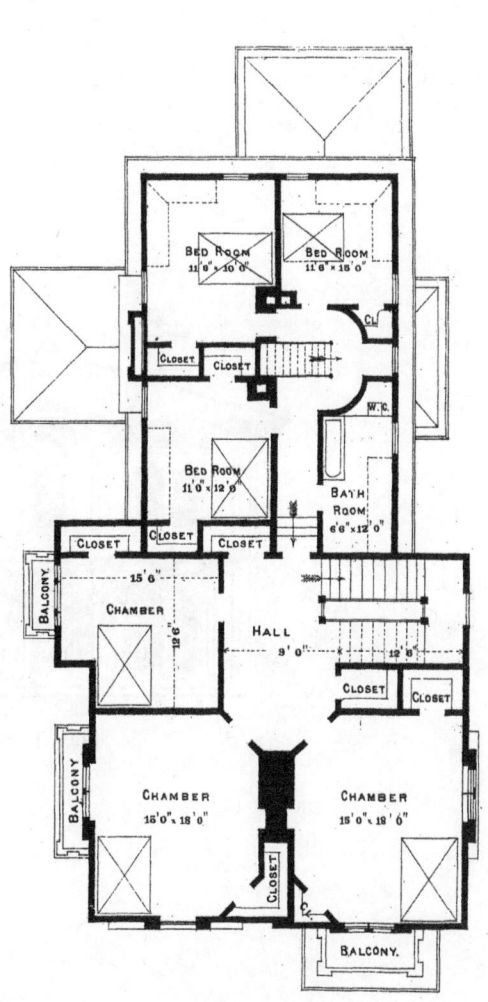

SECOND STORY PLAN

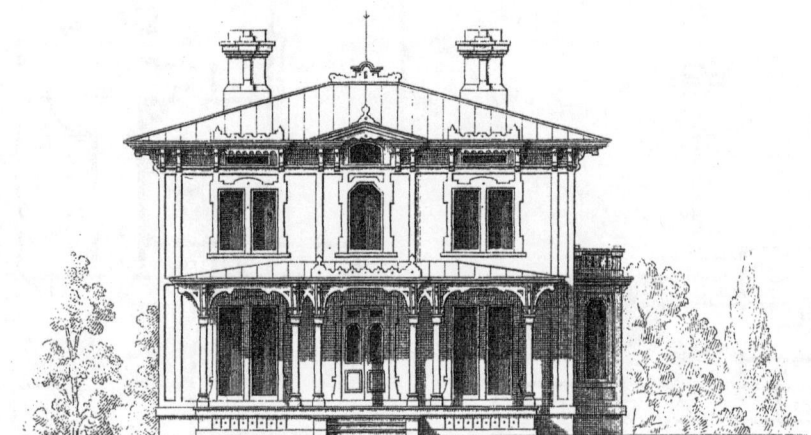

FRONT ELEVATION

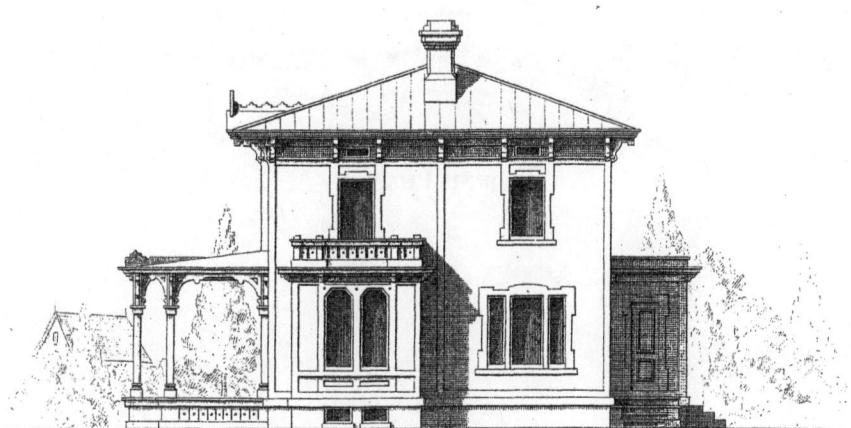

SIDE ELEVATION.

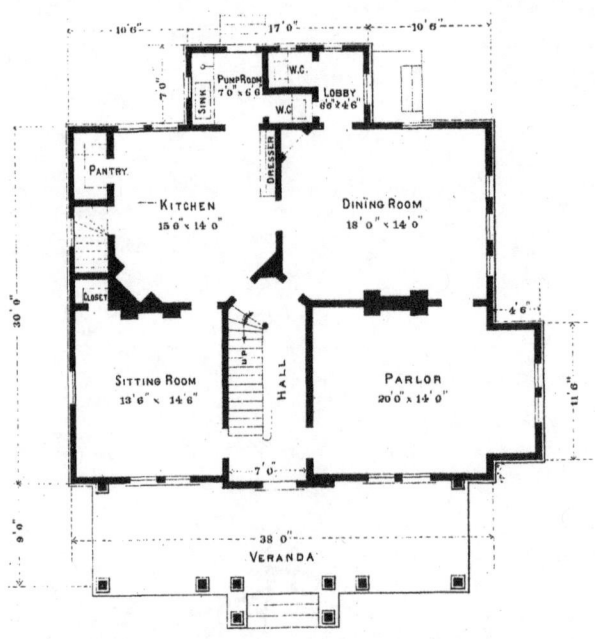

GROUND PLAN.

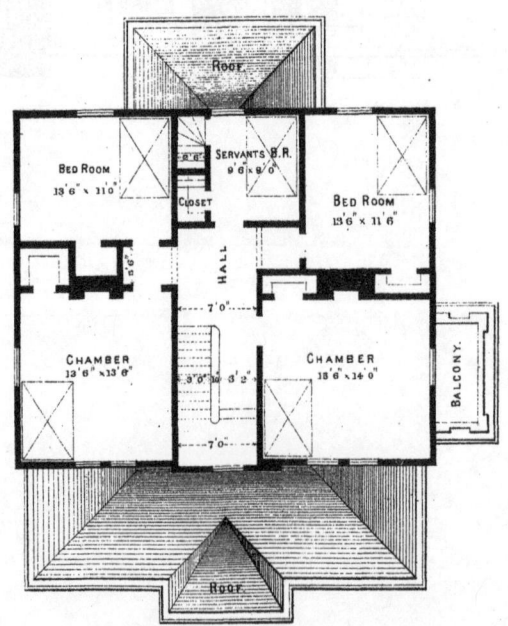

CHAMBER PLAN.

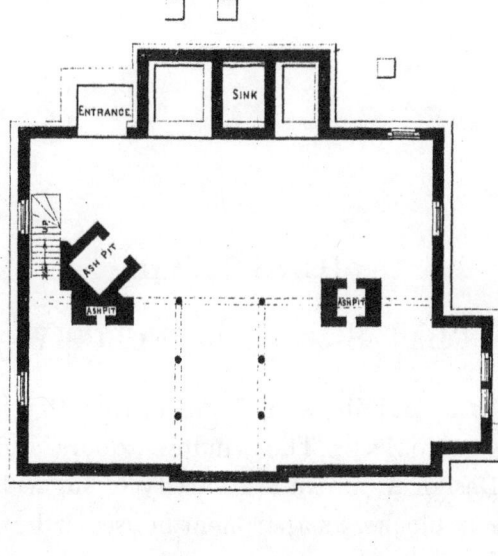

CELLAR PLAN.

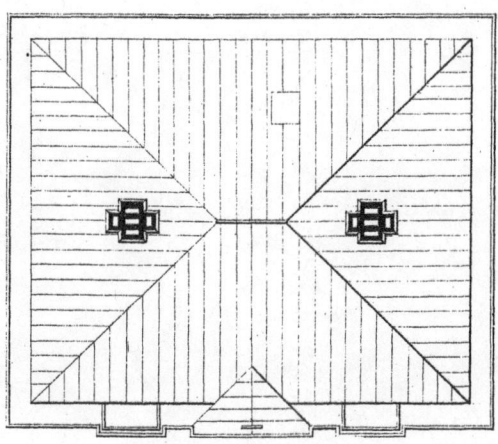

ROOF PLAN.

DESIGN H.

PLATES 33 TO 40, INCLUSIVE.

This design for a block of buildings, is distinct from that given in Plates one to eight, although designed for the same object. The windows, doors and all details are entirely distinct. There is here, as in Design A, an endless variety of suggestions for every description of city houses, either single or in blocks, as apartment houses or hotels, and for libraries, schools, or public buildings for use in villages.

PLATE 33.

DESIGN. H.

STREET ELEVATION

28"

10'0"

4'2"

2'6"

10"
13"

8'0"

5'8"

18"

10"
12"

8'9"

6'4"

18"

11"
13"

10'6"

7'6"

2'0"

10"
14"

9'0"

6'8"

18"

9"
12"

7'6"

2'0"

3'0"

3'7"

23'2"

— AVENUE ELEVATION —

SCALE ⅛ IN   Feet

1 2 3 4 5 6 7 8 9 10   15   20

0

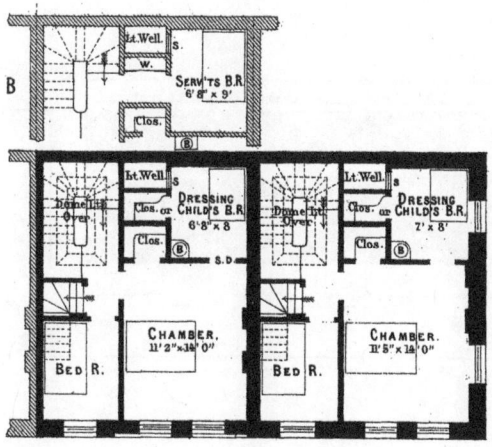

SECOND CHAMBER FLOOR

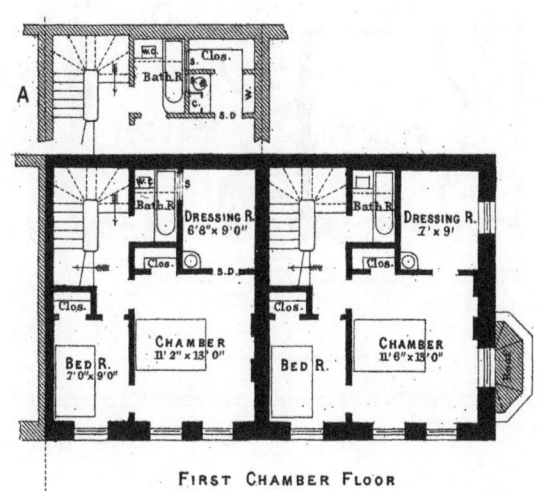

FIRST CHAMBER FLOOR

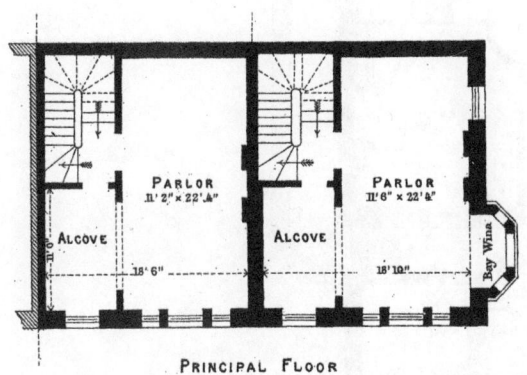

PRINCIPAL FLOOR

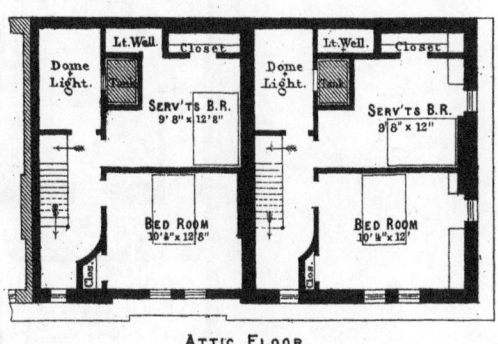

ATTIC FLOOR

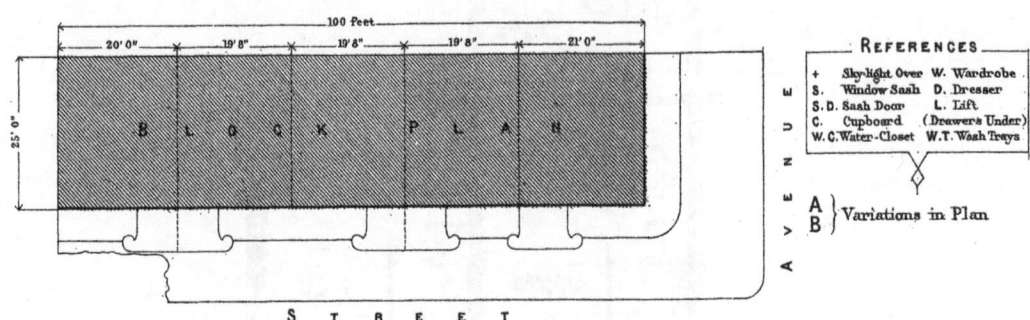

BLOCK PLAN

100 Feet

20'0" — 19'8" — 19'8" — 19'8" — 21'0"

25'0"

AVENUE

STREET

REFERENCES

+	Sky-light Over	W.	Wardrobe
S.	Window Sash	D.	Dresser
S.D.	Sash Door	L.	Lift
C.	Cupboard	(Drawers Under)
W.C.	Water-Closet	W.T.	Wash Trays

A
B } Variations in Plan

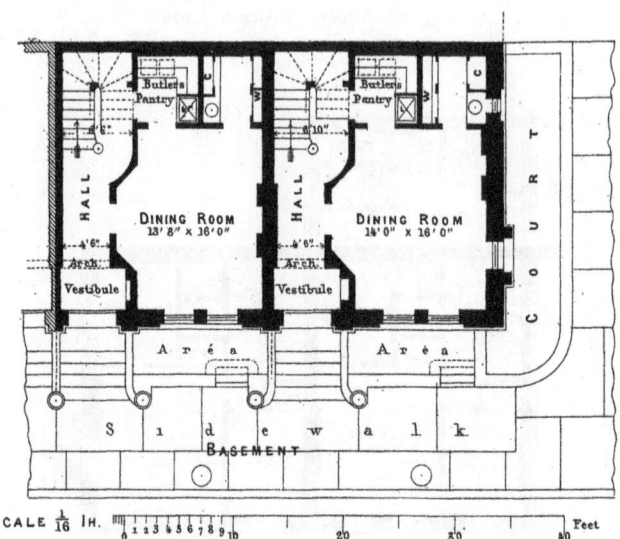

Butler's Pantry — DINING ROOM 13'8" x 16'0" — HALL — Vestibule — Area

Butler's Pantry — DINING ROOM 14'0" x 16'0" — HALL — Vestibule — Area

COURT

Area

Area

Sidewalk

BASEMENT

SCALE 1/16 IH.   0 1 2 3 4 5 6 7 8 9 10   20   30   40 Feet

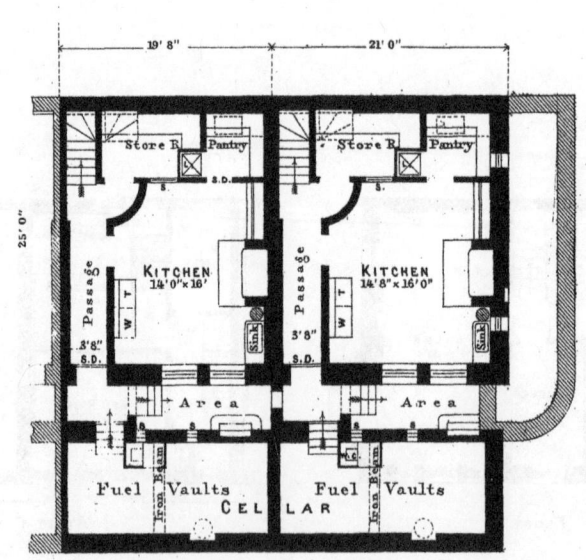

19'8"   21'0"

25'0"

Store R. — Pantry — KITCHEN 14'0" x 18' — Passage — W.T — Sink

Store R. — Pantry — KITCHEN 14'8" x 16'0" — Passage — W.T — Sink

Area

Area

Fuel Vaults   Iron Beam   CELLAR   Fuel Vaults   Iron Beam

42

SCALE ⅜ In

Feet

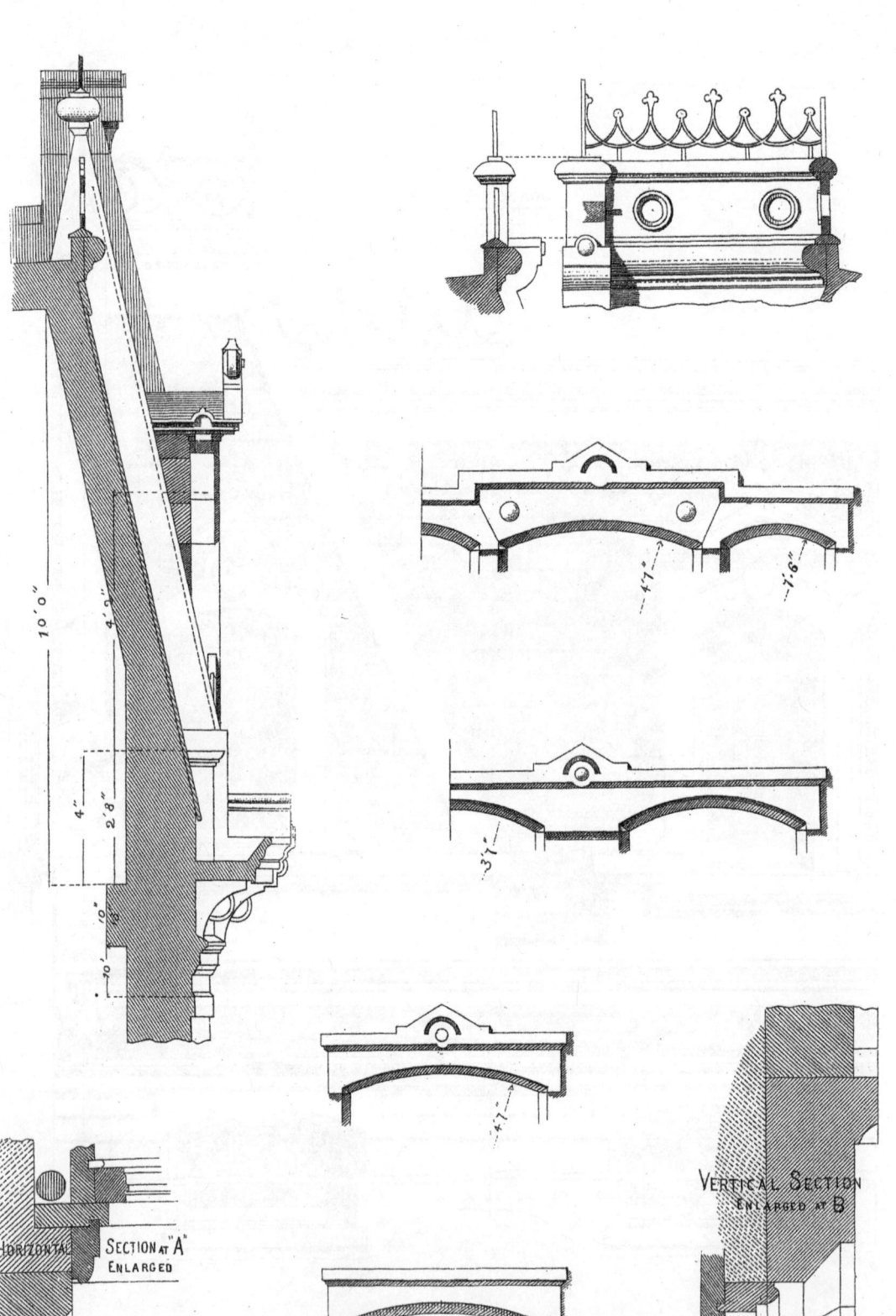

HORIZONTAL SECTION AT "A" ENLARGED

VERTICAL SECTION ENLARGED AT B

A

SCALE ⅜ IN

B

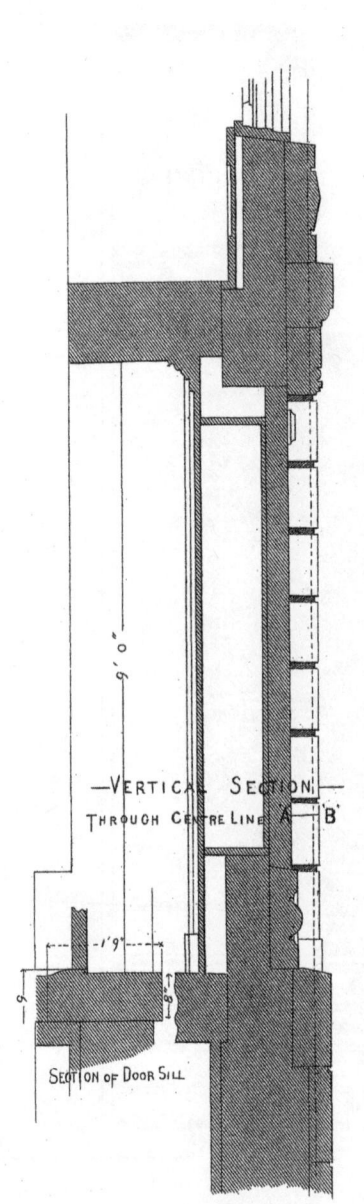

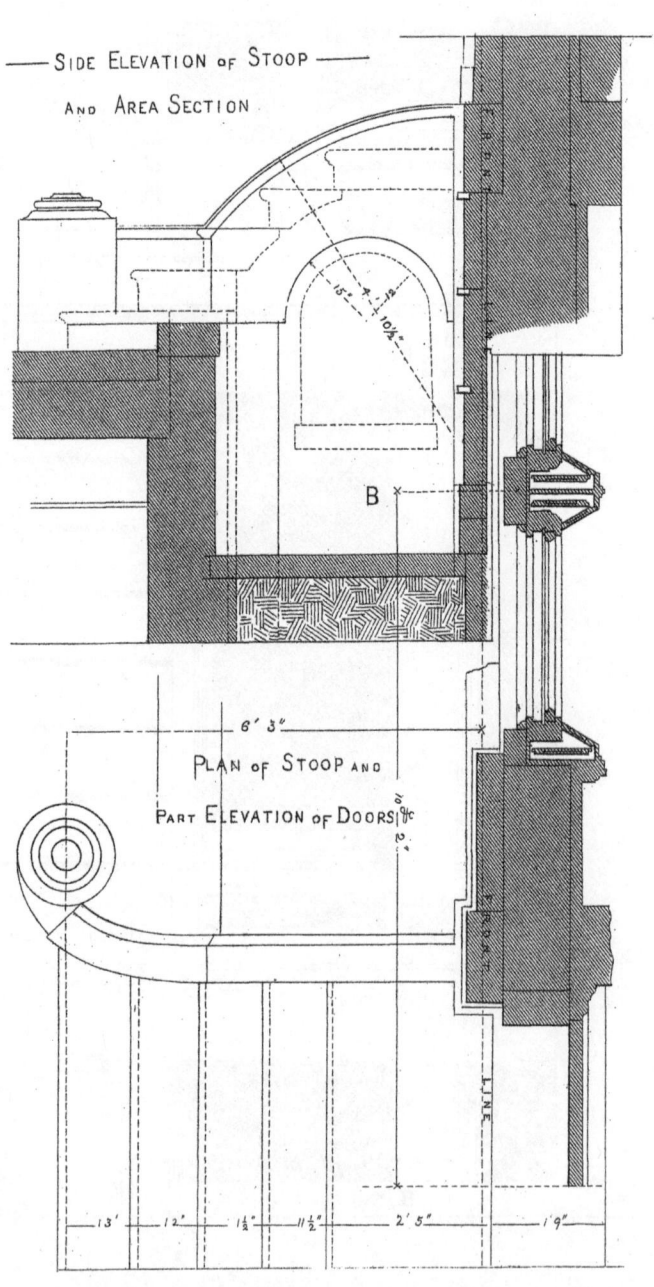

SIDE ELEVATION OF STOOP

AND AREA SECTION

B

PLAN OF STOOP AND

PART ELEVATION OF DOORS &c.

9'. 0"

VERTICAL SECTION

THROUGH CENTRE LINE A — B'

1' 9"

9"

SECTION OF DOOR SILL

6' 3"

13'   12"   1½"   11½"   2' 5"   1' 9"

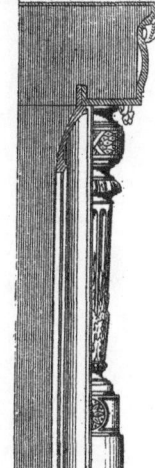

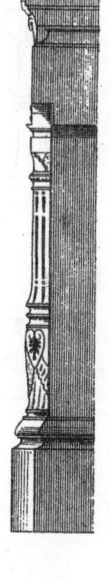

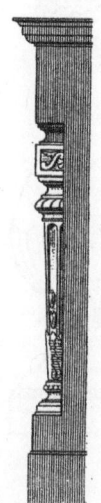

Chas. Hart. Lith. 36 Vesey St. N.Y.

Chas.Hart.Lith. 36 Vesey St.N.Y.

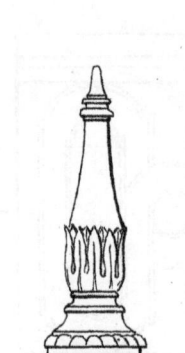
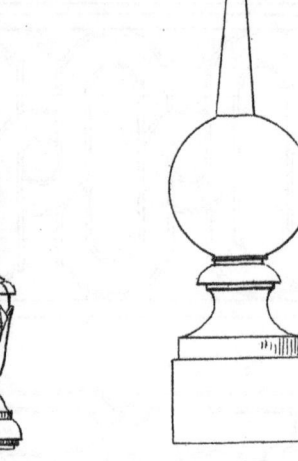

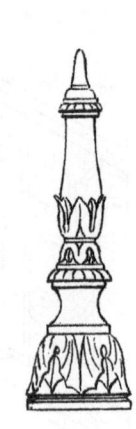

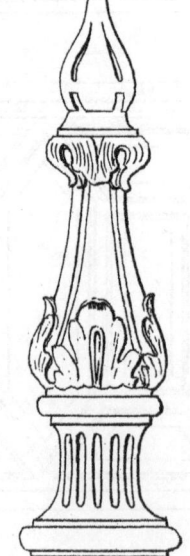
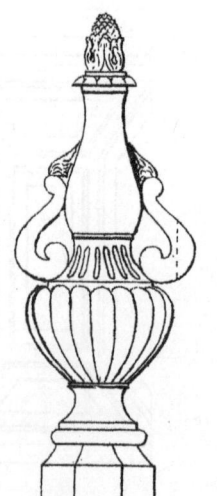

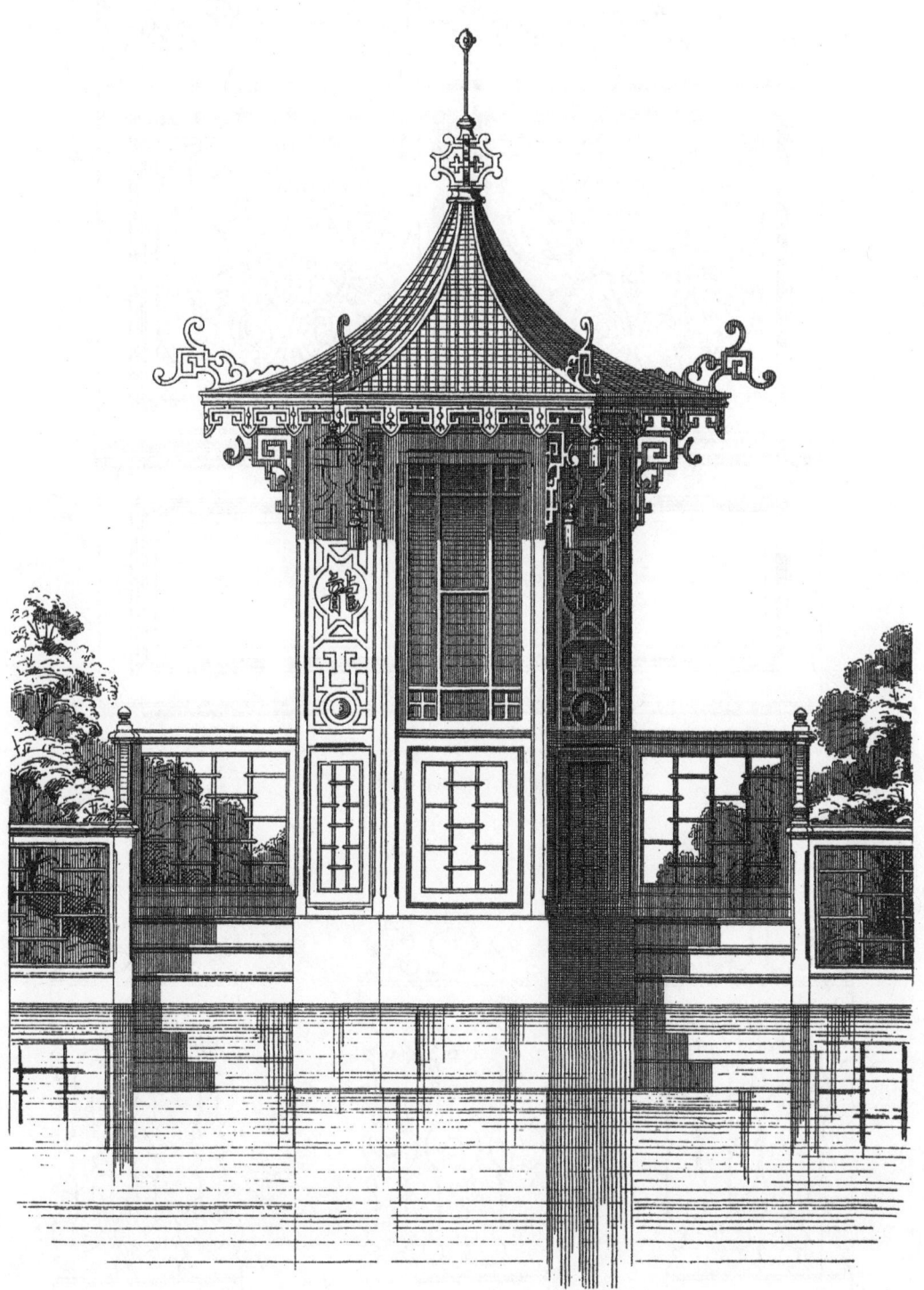

BOAT LANDING

OFFICE PARTITION

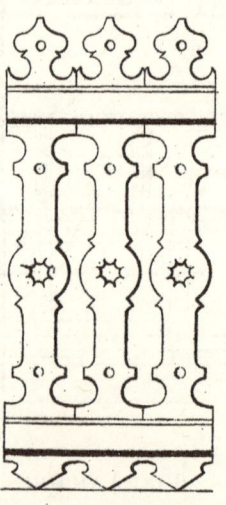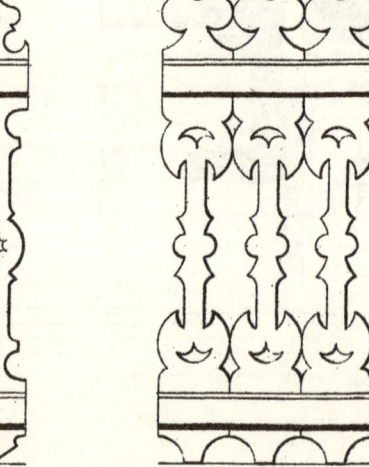

DESIGNS FOR FENCES

Scale Two Feet to an inch

DESIGN FOR A SUMMER HOUSE

OFFICE PARTITION

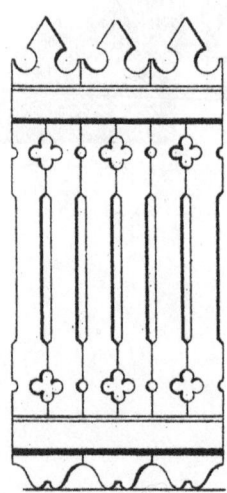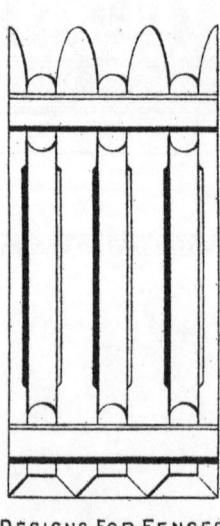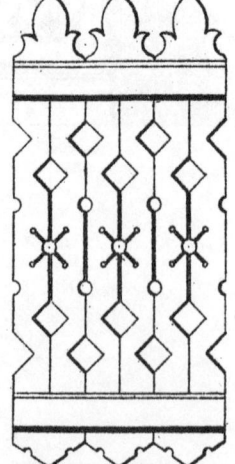

DESIGNS FOR FENCES

CAMPANILE FOR A FARM BARN

VERANDA

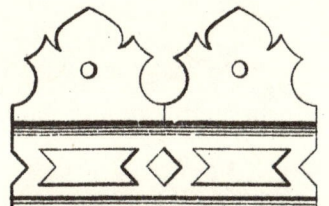
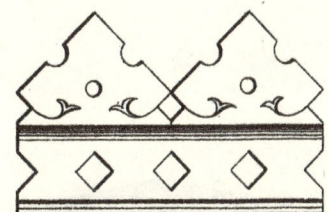
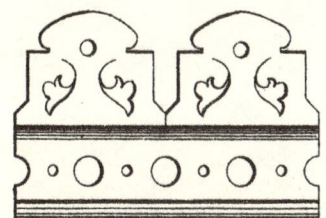

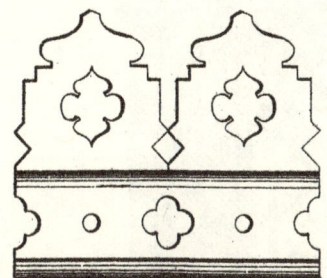

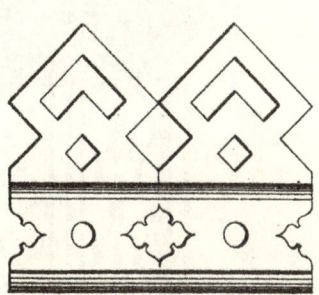

CRESTING FOR ROOFS

ORIEL WINDOW

DESIGN K.

PLATES 57 to 64, INCLUSIVE.

This design is for a city house with a rear extention, to be erected on a lot twenty-five feet wide. The Bay window in the rear is designed without inside shutters, the sash being intended to be heavily curtained, and the sliding doors will effectually shut off colds and draughts. The position of the Bay at the rear of the house will usually prevent much exposure to the sun, outside blinds or inside shutters can, of course, with slight modifications, be used. The rail on front steps can be made of any of the usual patterns; it is left out of the drawing in order to show more clearly the front outline of the steps.

The details of Butlers pantry and the Bay window are very full and clear.

HEIGHTS

FRONT ELEVATION

SCALE

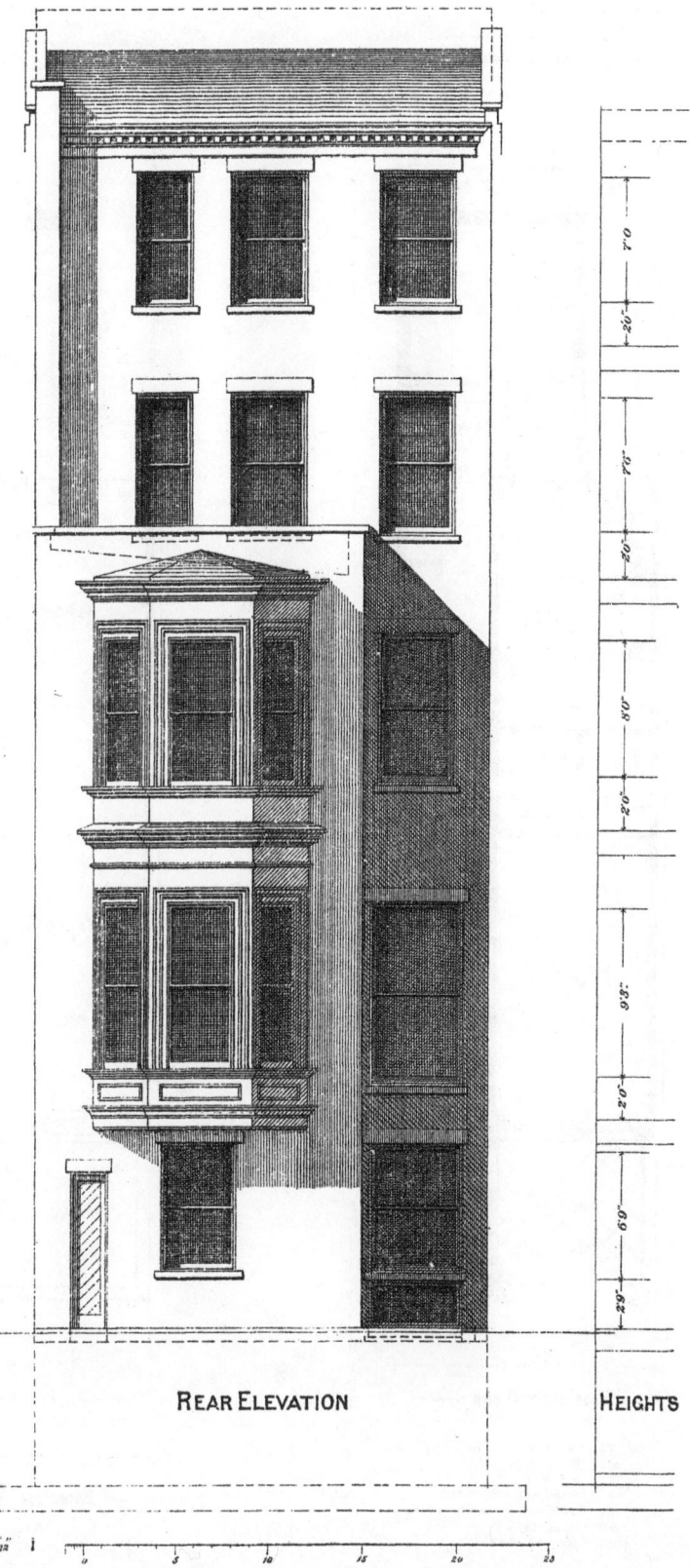

REAR ELEVATION

HEIGHTS

SCALE ³⁄₃₂ 1   0   5   10   15   20   25

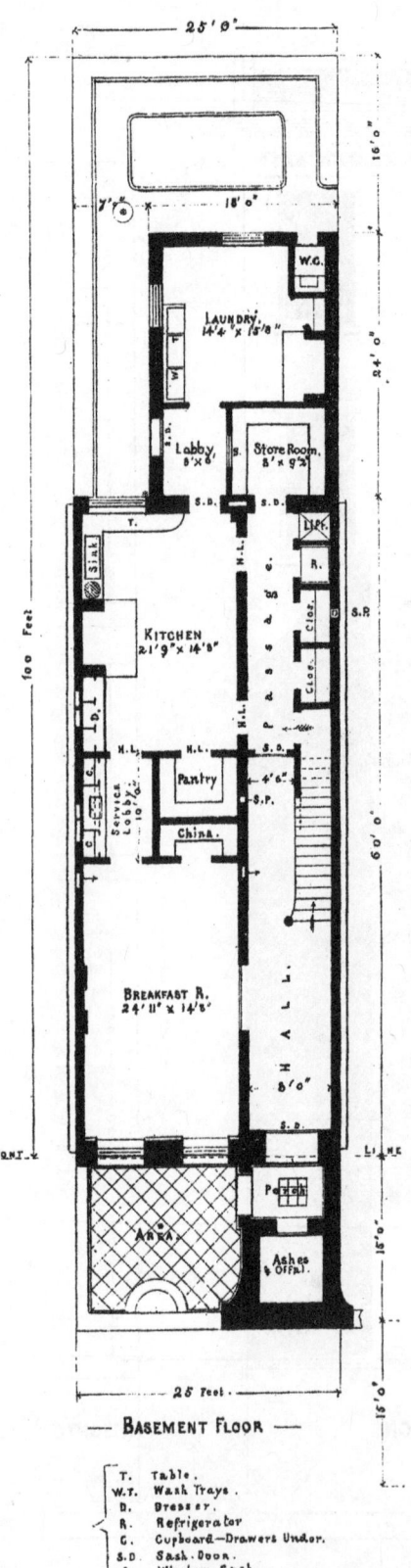

— BASEMENT FLOOR —

T.   Table.
W.T.   Wash Trays.
D.   Dresser.
R.   Refrigerator.
C.   Cupboard—Drawers Under.
S.D.   Sash Door.
S.   Window Sash.

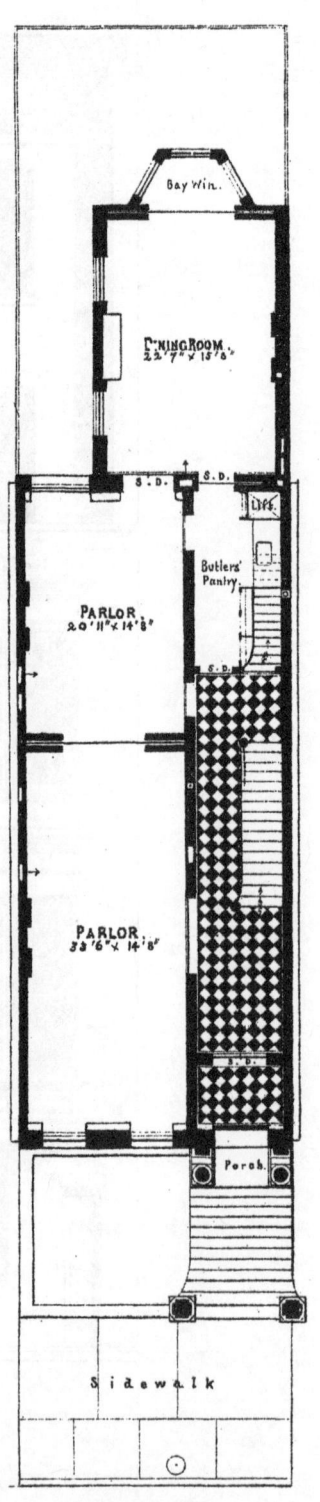

— PRINCIPAL FLOOR —

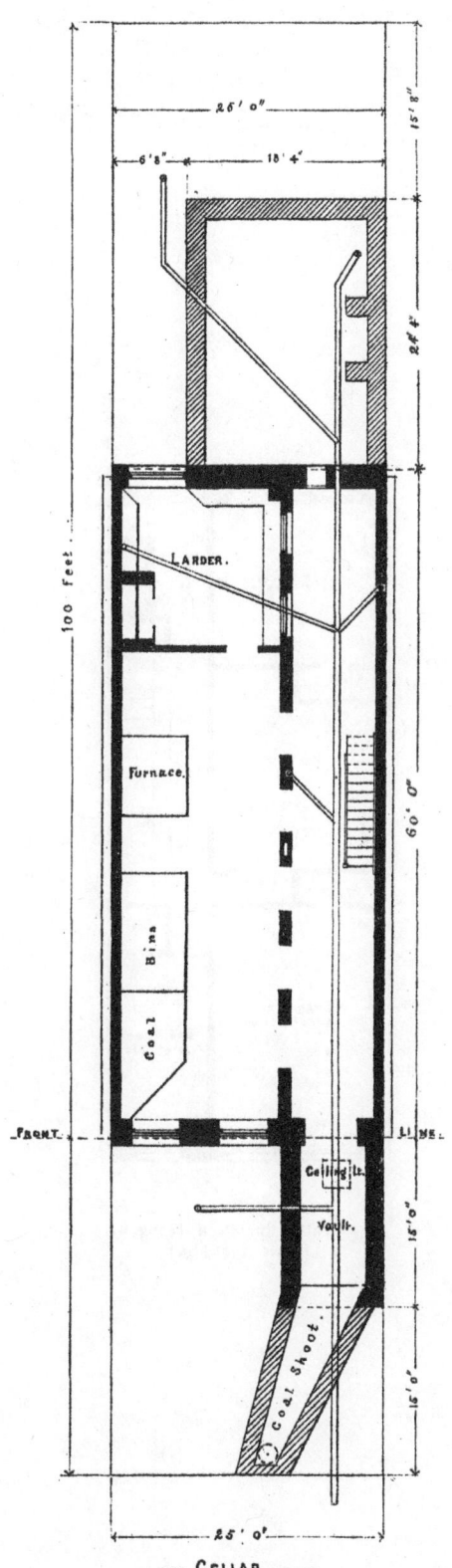

25' 0"

6'8"   18'4"

15'8"

24'4"

100 Feet.

LARDER.

60' 0"

Furnace.

Coal Bins

FRONT.   LINE.

Ceiling Lt.

Vault.

15' 0"

15' 0"

Coal Shoot.

25' 0"

— CELLAR. —

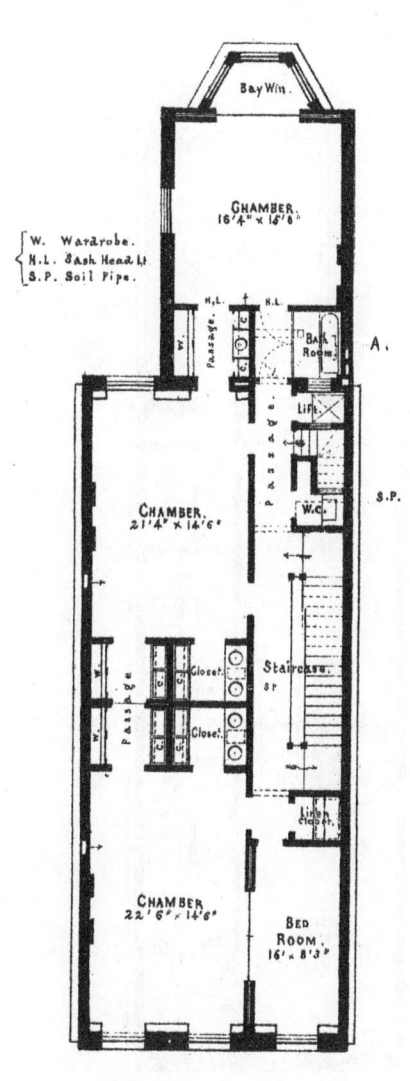

Bay Win.

CHAMBER.
16'4" x 15'8"

W. Wardrobe.
H.L. Sash Head Lt.
S.P. Soil Pipe.

H.L.   H.L.

W.   Bath
             Room   A.

Passage.   Lift

CHAMBER.
21'4" x 14'6"   W.C.   S.P.

Passage.   Closet.   Staircase.

W.   Closet.

Linen
Closet.

CHAMBER
22'6" x 14'6"   BED
                       ROOM
                       16' x 8'3"

— FIRST CHAMBER FLOOR —
(Doors 8'6" high

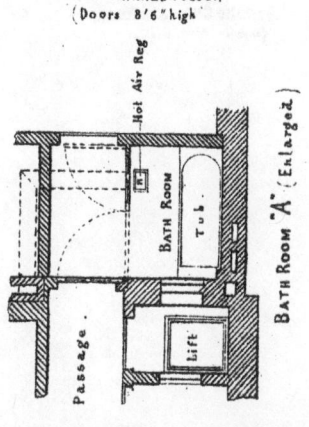

Hot Air Reg.

BATH ROOM
Tub.

Passage.   Lift

BATH ROOM "A" (Enlarged.)

SCALE ⅟₁₆ Inch.   1 2 3 4   5   6 7 8 9   10   15   20   25   30   Feet.

W.   Wardrobe.
C.   Cupboard (Drawers under)
+ .   Sky-Light Over
H.L. Head-light.

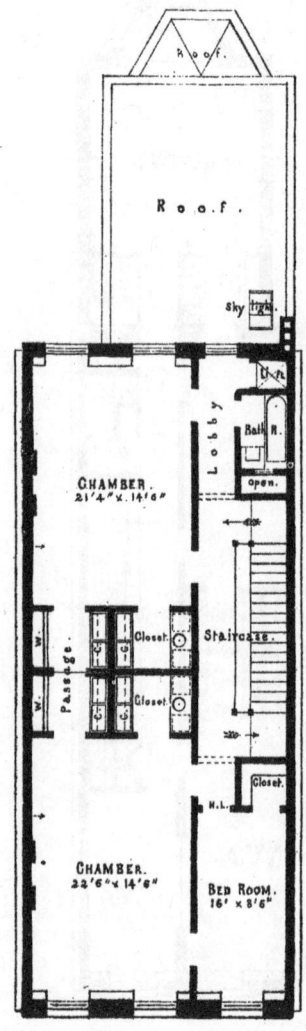

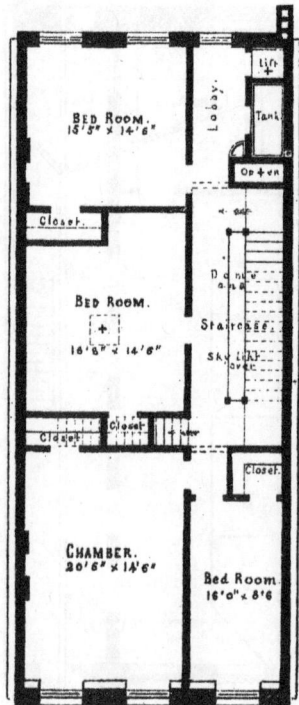

— SECOND CHAMBER FLOOR —
(Doors 8'0" high.)

—THIRD CHAMBER FLOOR.—
(Doors 7'6" high)

SCALE ⅟₁₆ Inch   Feet.

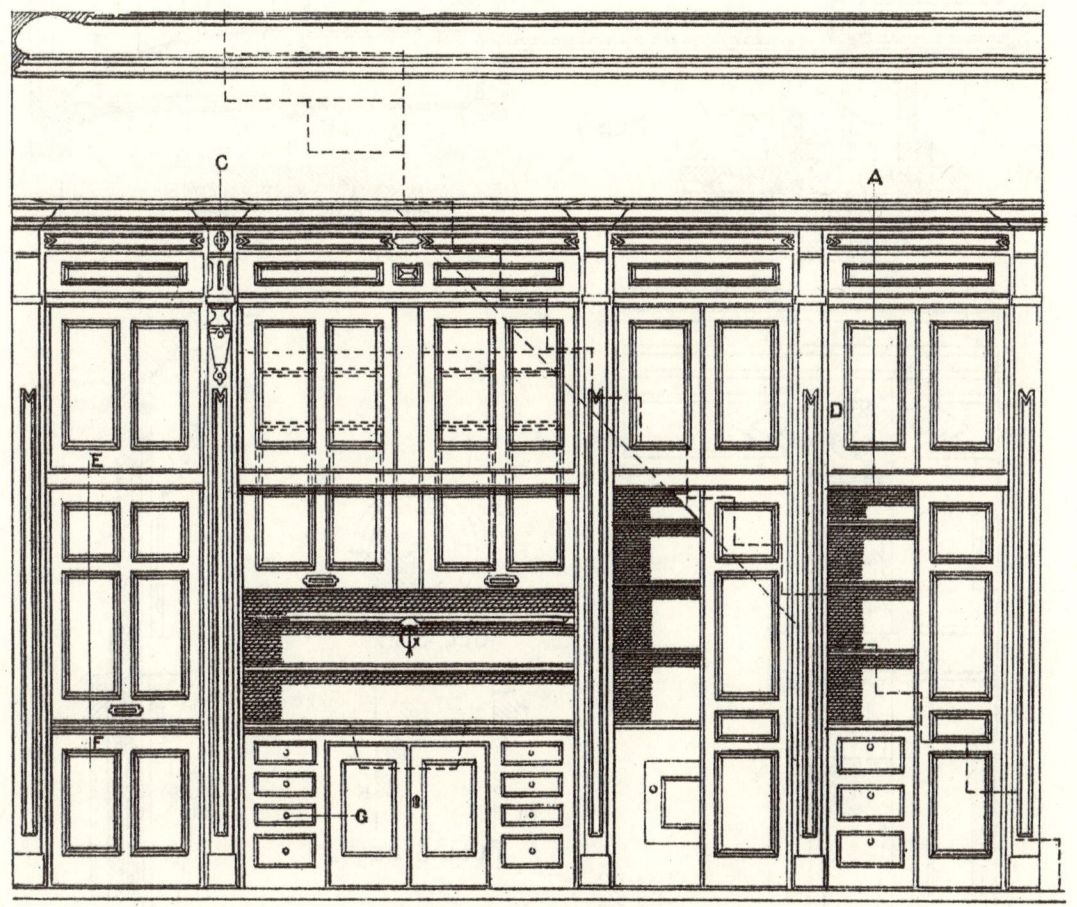

ELEVATION, BUTLER'S PANTRY

DETAILS, BUTLERS' PANTRY.

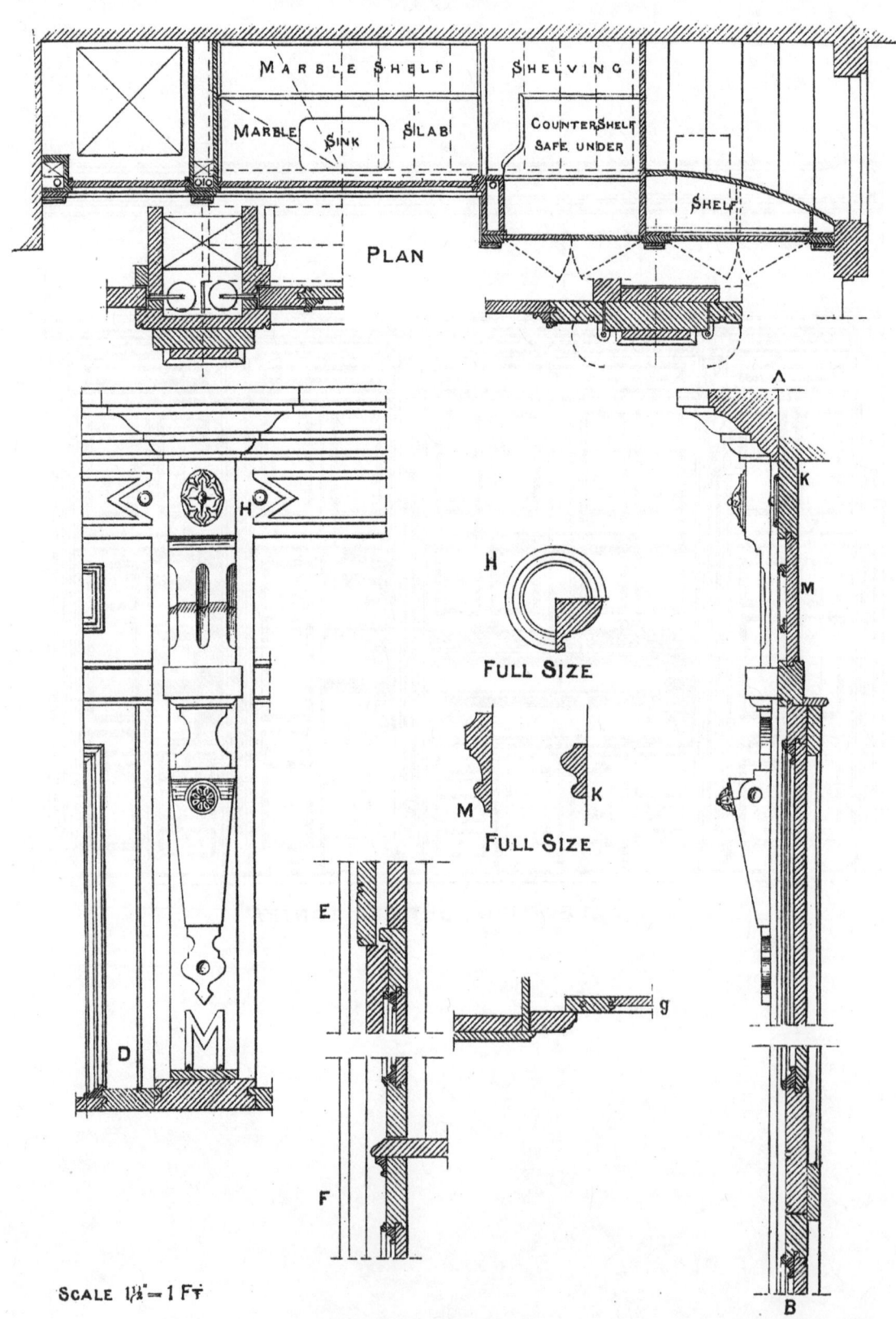

MARBLE SHELF   SHELVING

MARBLE   SINK   SLAB

COUNTER SHELF
SAFE UNDER

SHELF

PLAN

H

FULL SIZE

M   K

FULL SIZE

H

D   M

E

F

g

A

K

M

B

SCALE 1½" = 1 FT

DETAILS of BAY WINDOW

REAR ELEVATION

DINING R. ELEVATION
of SLIDING DOORS

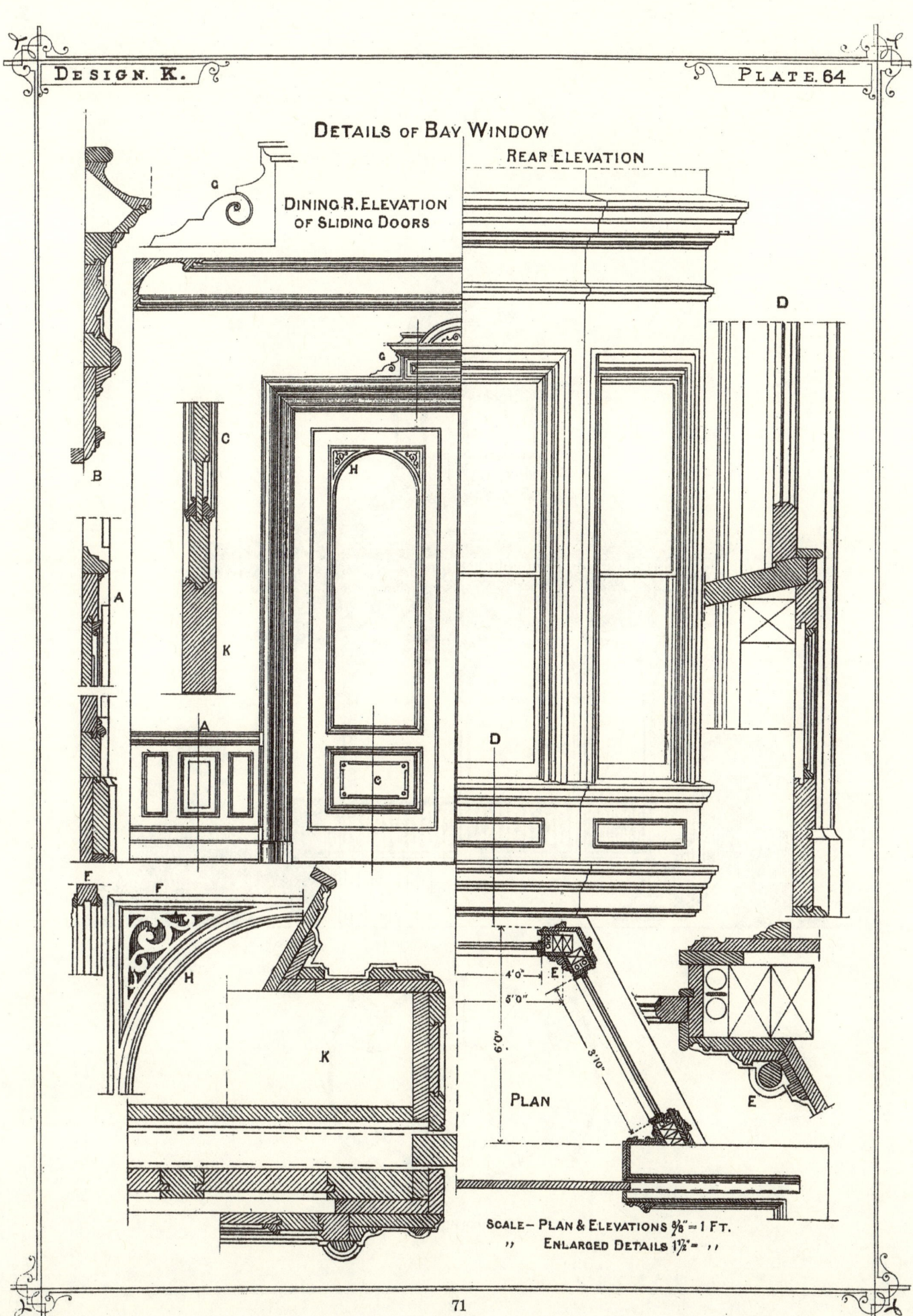

B

A

C

K

A

A

C

F

F

H

K

D

D

H

E

E

E

4'0"

5'0"

6'0"

3'10"

PLAN

SCALE— PLAN & ELEVATIONS ⅜"= 1 FT.
,,　　ENLARGED DETAILS 1½"= ,,

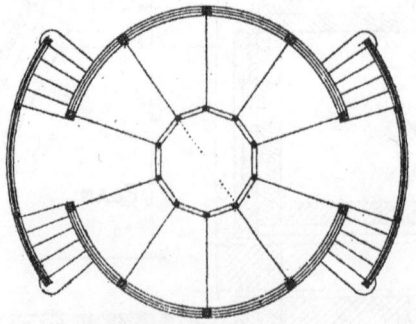

SUMMER HOUSE

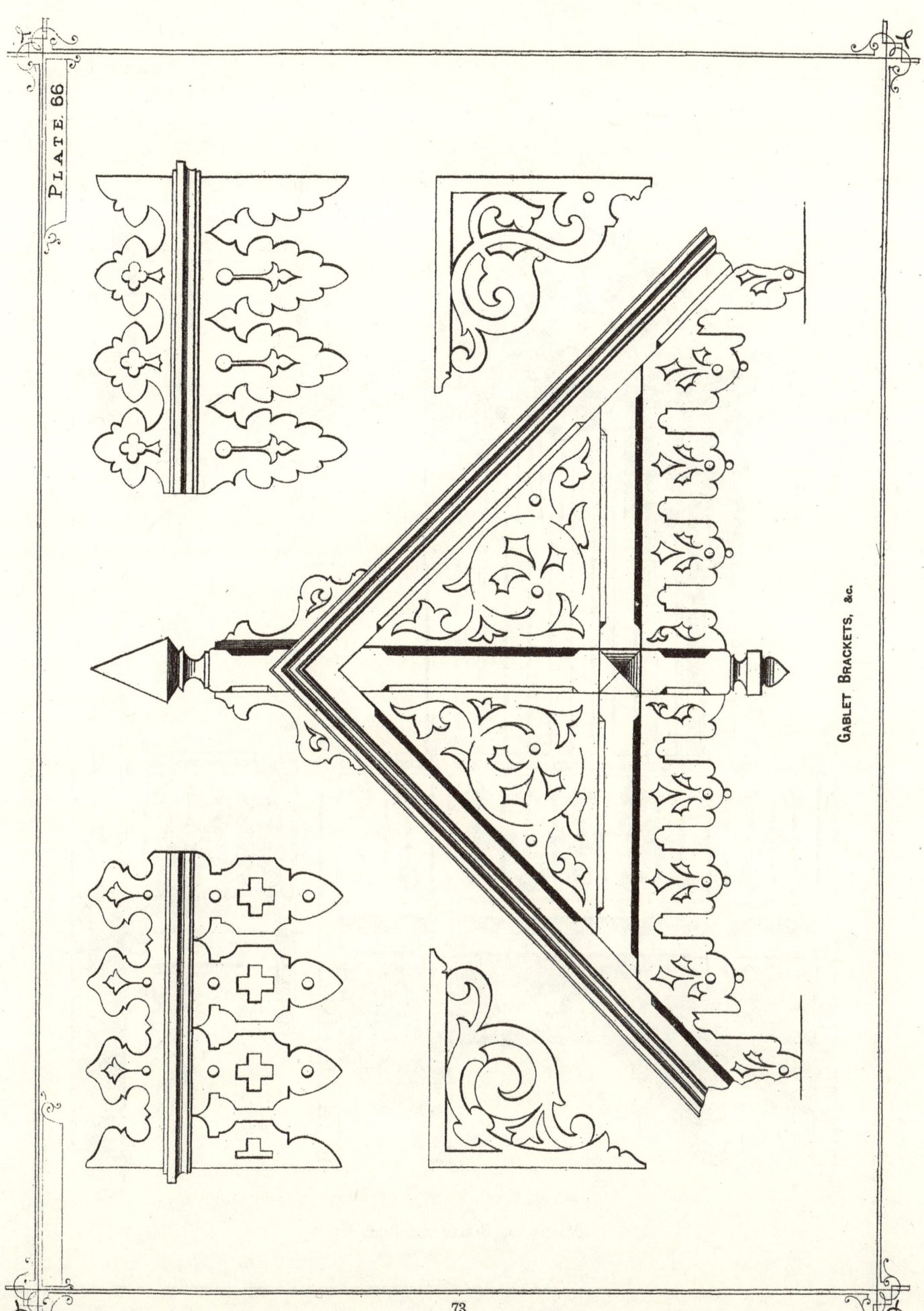

GABLET BRACKETS, &c.

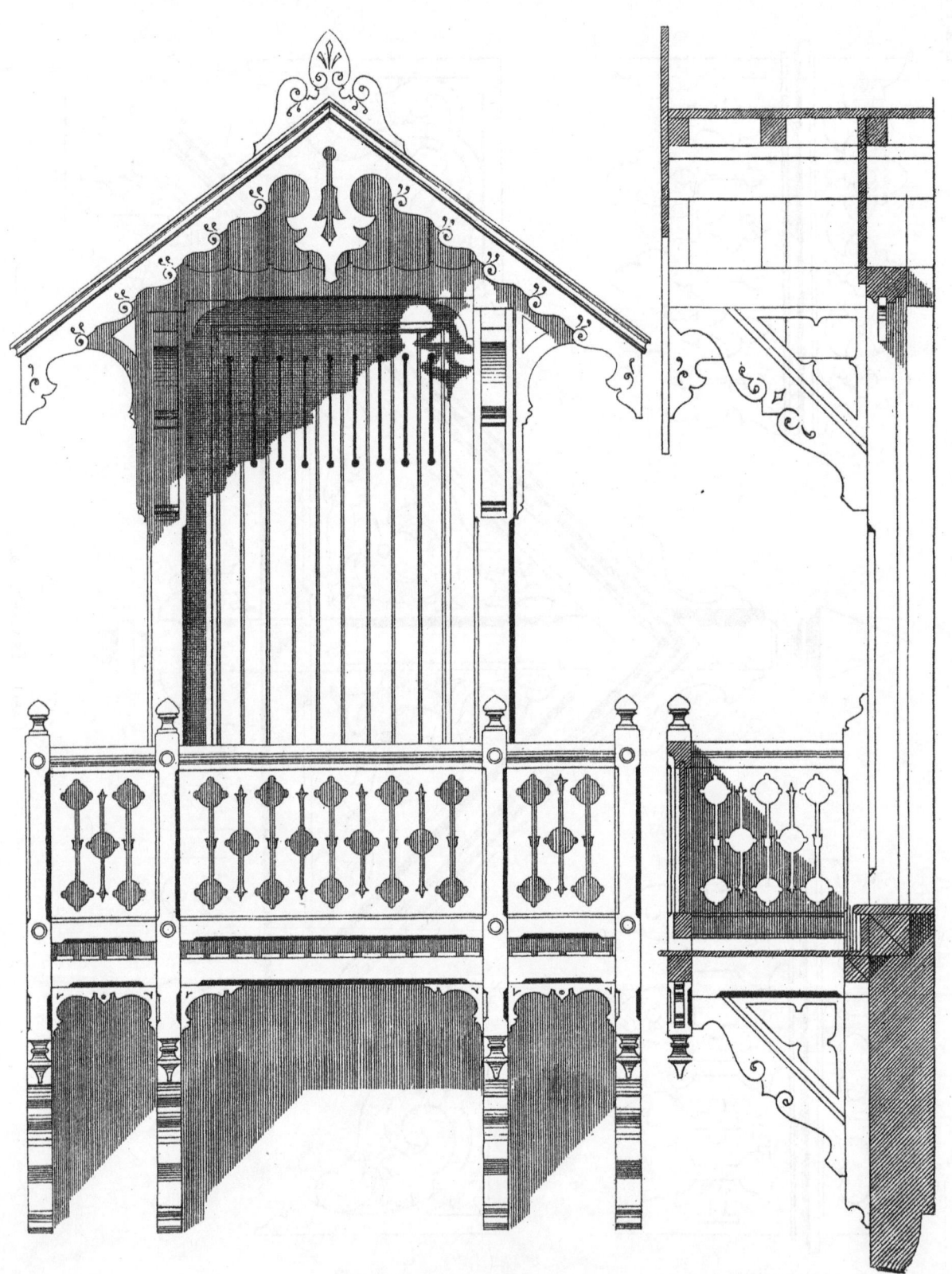

ORNAMENTAL GABLET FOR BARN.

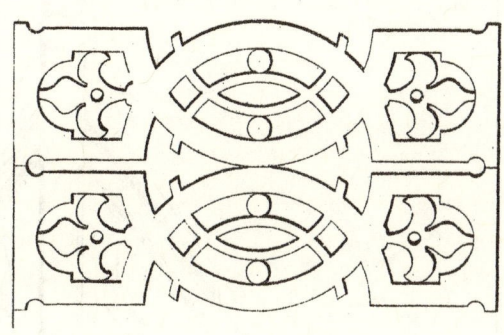
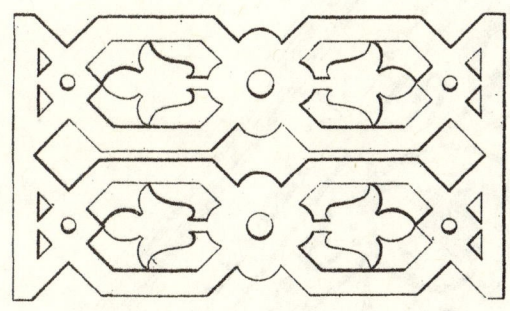

BALUSTRADES AND PANELS.

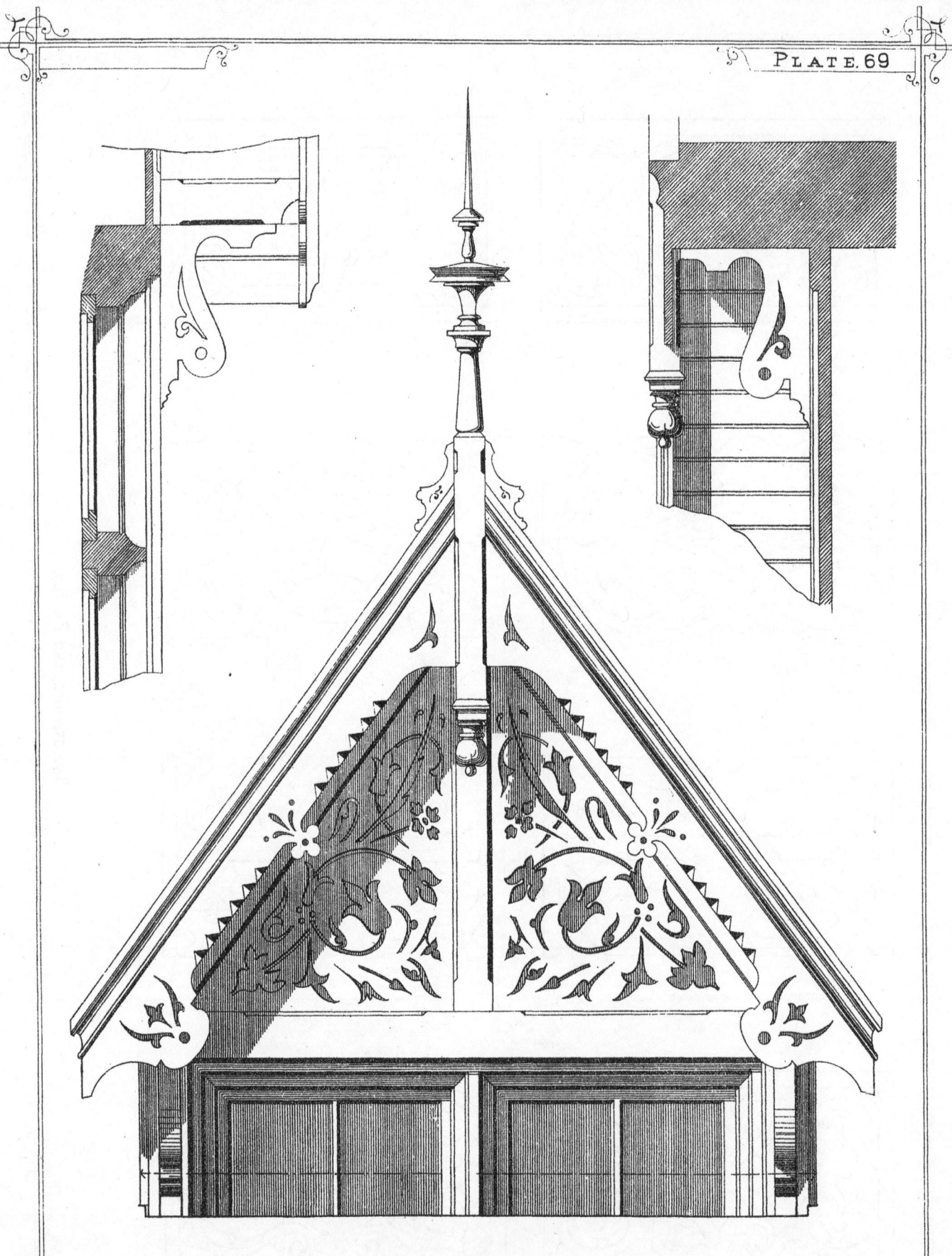

ORNAMENTAL HOOD.

Cresting For Roofs

FINIALS.

Plate 72

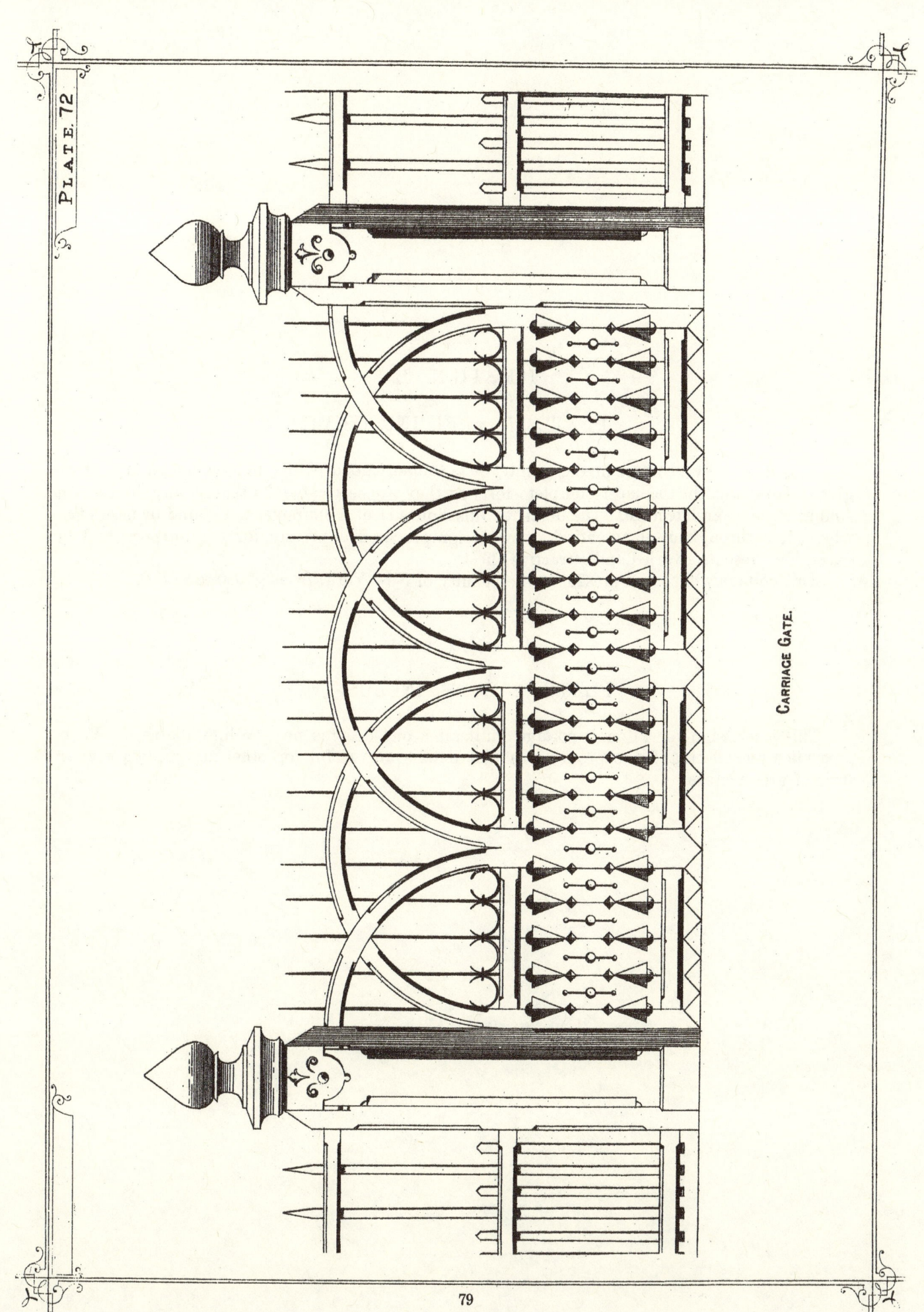

Carriage Gate.

DESIGN L.

PLATES 73 TO 84, INCLUSIVE.

This design for a cottage in the country has so many good points to recommend it that we give the drawings in the most complete form as they are servicable for almost any house of a similar style of architecture. The detail of this house is of a character not found or used elsewhere, it is throughout of an entirely new design prepared expressly for the purpose, and in execution presents a varied and attractive effect.

This cottage will cost at present in the vicinity of New York, from $4,000 to $4,500.

DESIGN M.

PLATES 85 TO 88, INCLUSIVE.

This is a design for a double cottage built after our designs near White Plains, N. Y., it presents a fine effect, and the proportions and details are useful for other designs of a similar style of architecture.

FRONT ELEVATION

SCALE ⅛"=1'

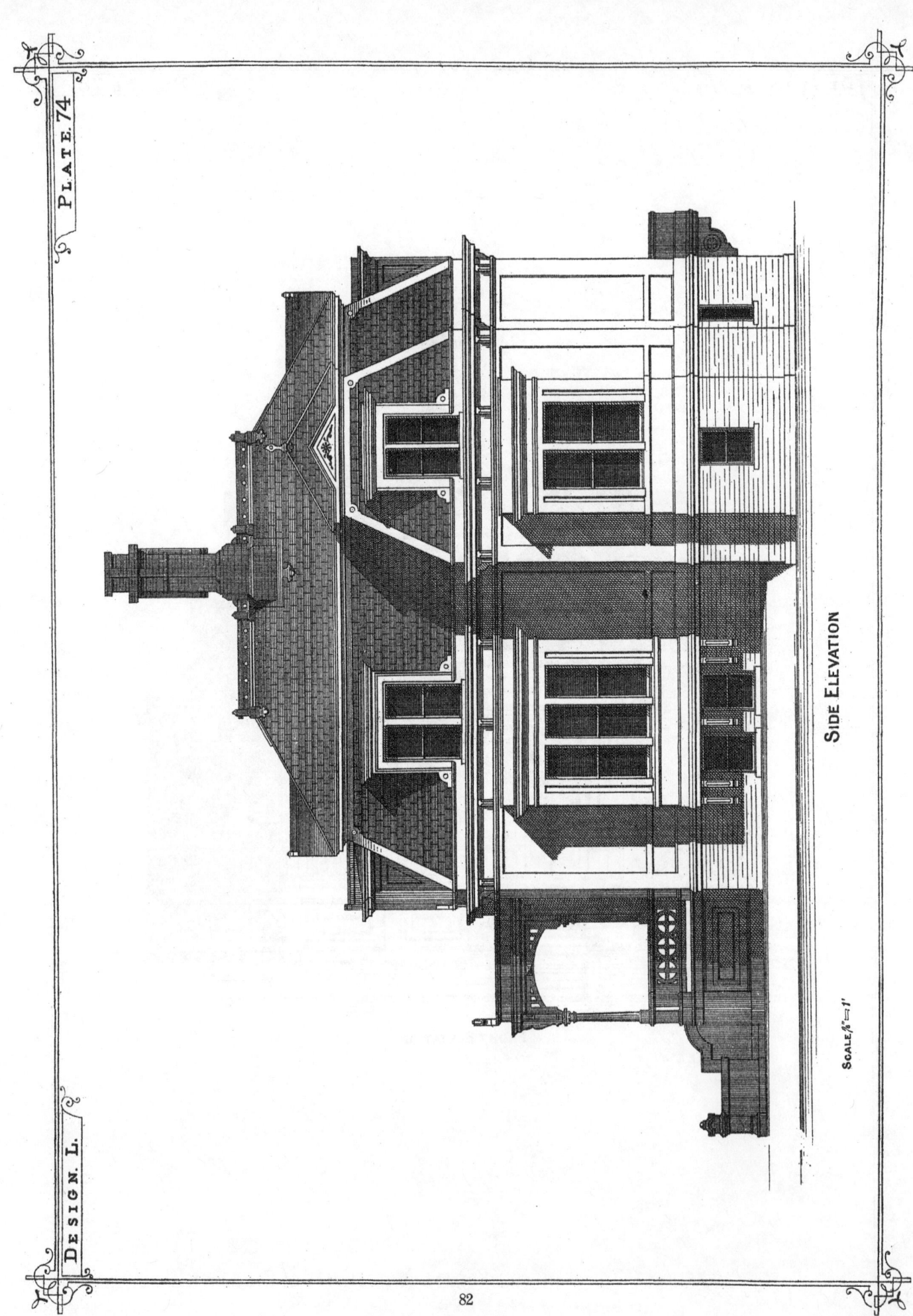

SIDE ELEVATION

SCALE ⅛"=1'

PLATE. 74

DESIGN. L.

REAR ELEVATION.

SCALE ½ INCH TO THE FOOT

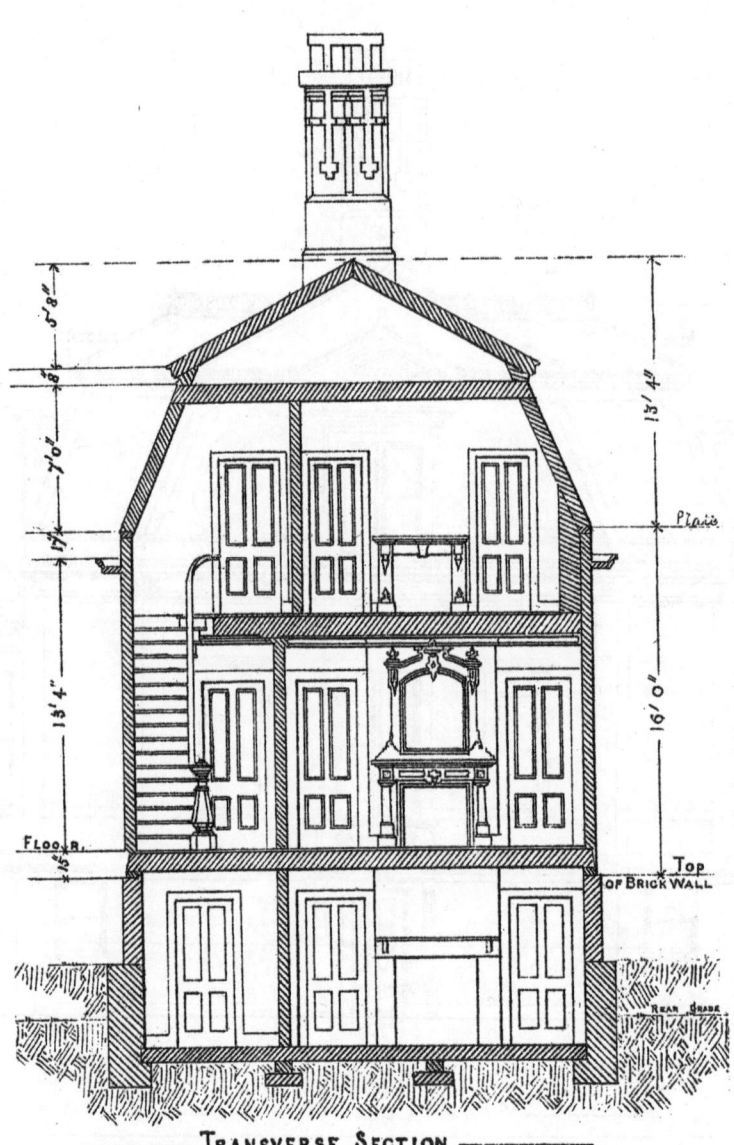

— TRANSVERSE SECTION —

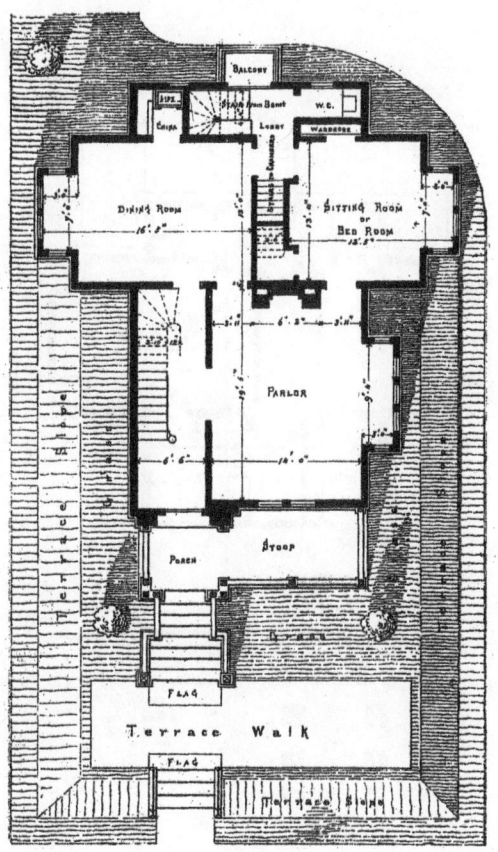

GROUND PLAN

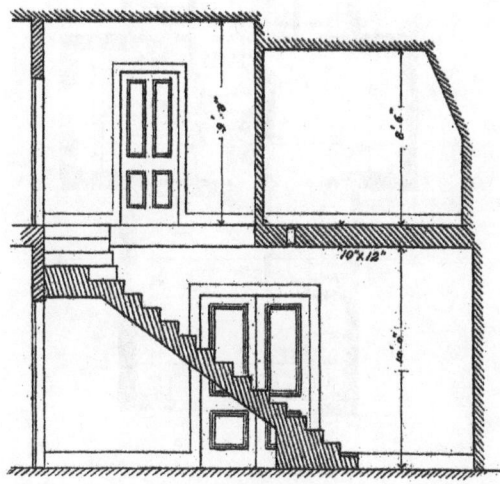

LONGITUDINAL SECTION

SCALE OF THE GROUND PLAN ⅟₁₆ INCH TO THE FOOT.   SCALE OF SECTION ⅛ INCH TO THE FOOT.

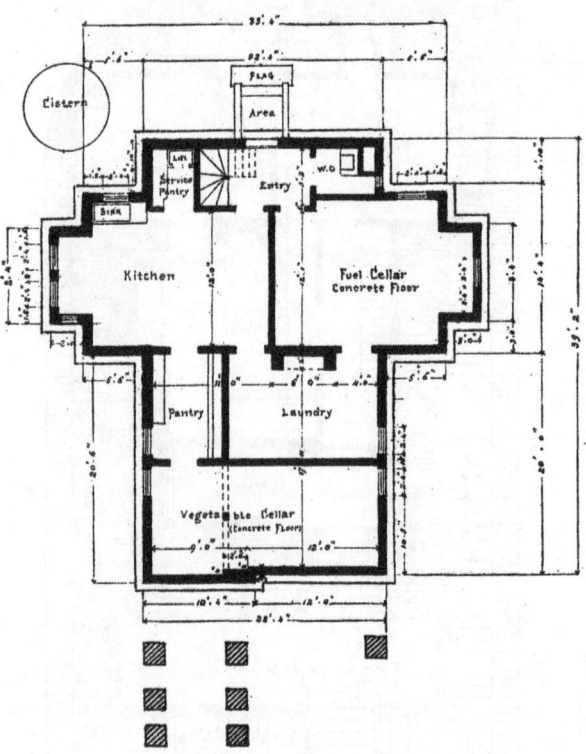

BASEMENT PLAN

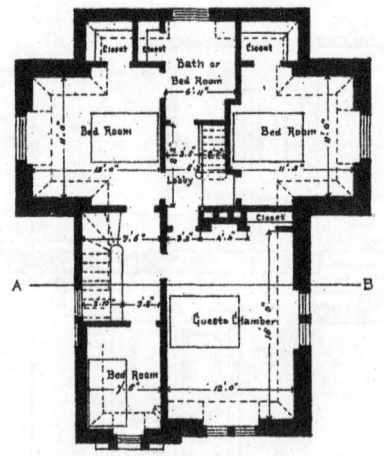

CHAMBER PLAN

SCALE 1/16 INCH TO THE FOOT.

CIRCULAR HD DORMER

SCALE ½ INCH TO THE FOOT

MAIN FRONT DORMER

SCALE ½ INCH TO THE FOOT

GABLE "F"

SCALE 1½ INCH TO THE FOOT

SIDE ELEVATION
OF
MAIN FRONT DORMER

SLATE

ROOF BOARD RAFTER

TONGUED SIDING

ROUGH BOARD

FACE OF BRACKET "B"

SECTION THROUGH "C D"

PROFILE OF BRACKET "B"

SCALE 1½ INCH TO THE FOOT

FINIAL "E"

"G"

SCALE 1 INCH TO THE FOOT

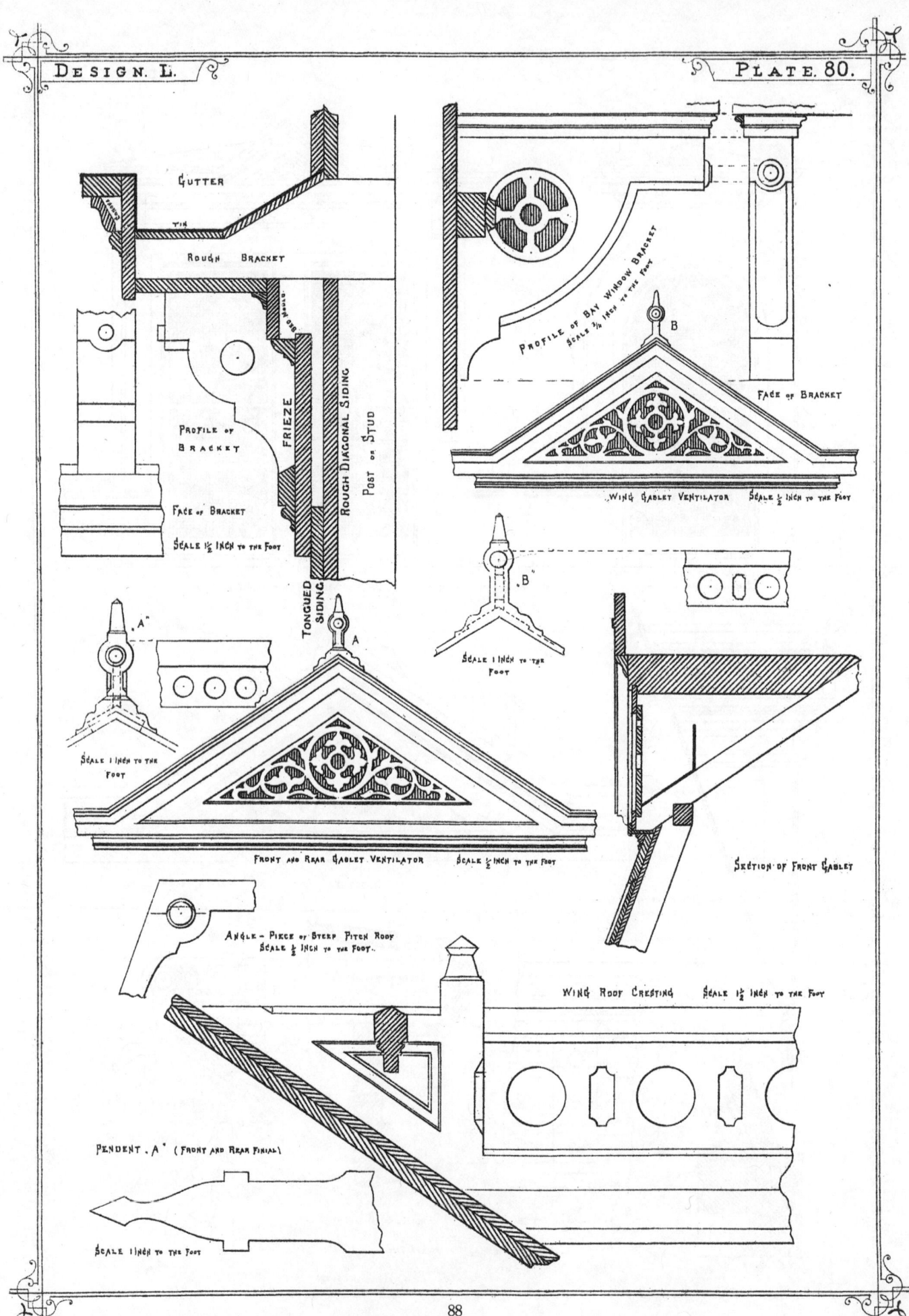

GUTTER

ROUGH BRACKET

PROFILE OF BRACKET

FRIEZE

ROUGH DIAGONAL SIDING

POST OR STUD

TONGUED SIDING

FACE OF BRACKET

SCALE 1½ INCH TO THE FOOT

PROFILE OF BAY WINDOW BRACKET
SCALE 3/4 INCH TO THE FOOT

FACE OF BRACKET

B

WING GABLET VENTILATOR   SCALE ½ INCH TO THE FOOT

"B"

SCALE 1 INCH TO THE FOOT

"A"

A

SCALE 1 INCH TO THE FOOT

SECTION OF FRONT GABLET

FRONT AND REAR GABLET VENTILATOR   SCALE ½ INCH TO THE FOOT

ANGLE - PIECE OF STEEP PITCH ROOF
SCALE ½ INCH TO THE FOOT.

WING ROOF CRESTING   SCALE 1½ INCH TO THE FOOT

PENDENT. A" (FRONT AND REAR FINIAL)

SCALE 1 INCH TO THE FOOT

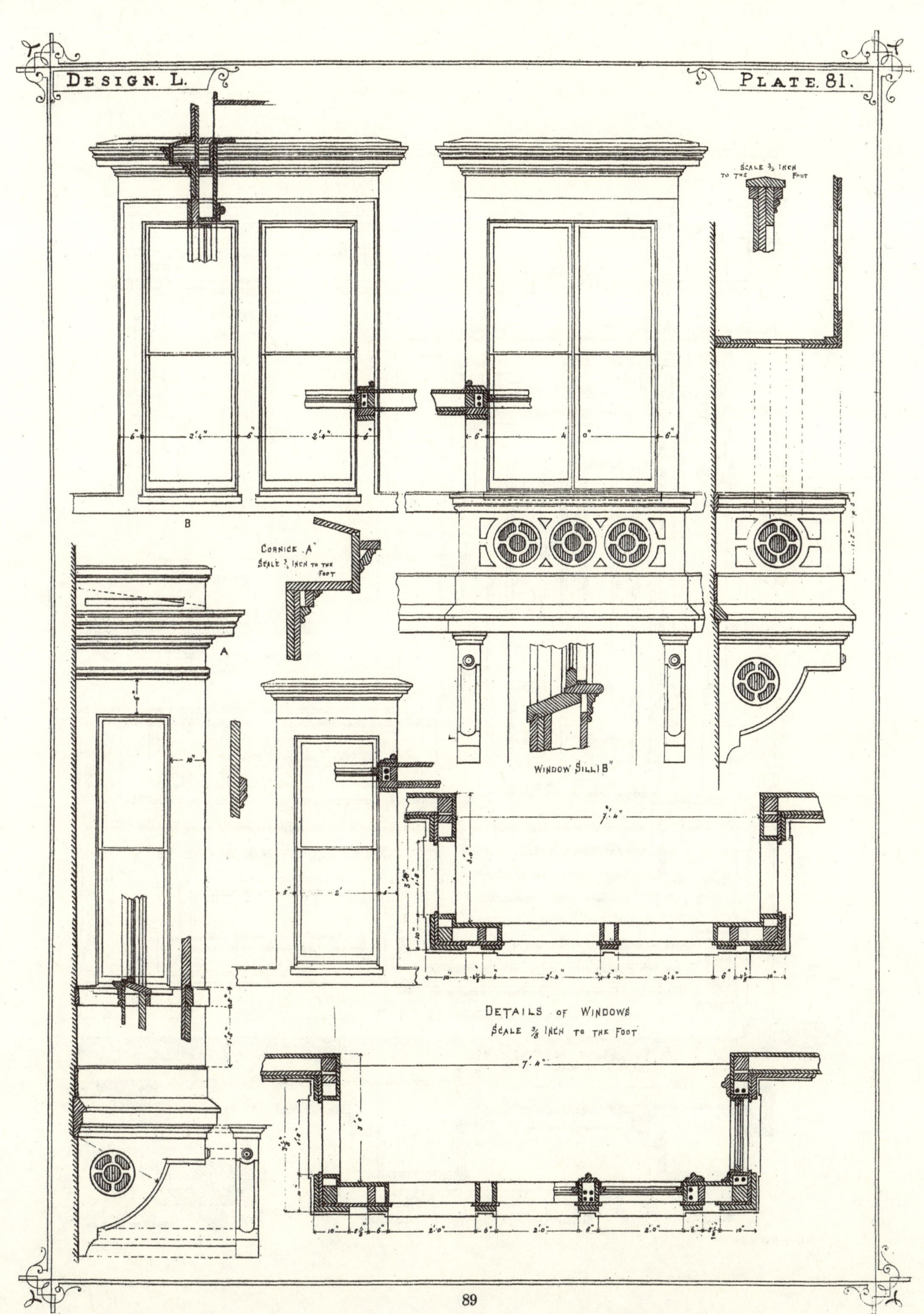

CORNICE "A"
SCALE ¾ INCH TO THE FOOT

WINDOW SILL B"

DETAILS OF WINDOWS
SCALE ⅜ INCH TO THE FOOT

ARCH BRACKET

PROFILE OF PORCH BRACKET

FOOT OF ARCH BRACKET

SCALE ¾ INCH TO THE FOOT

PANEL OF FRONT DOOR

SCALE 2 INCHES TO THE FOOT

GRADE LINE.

FRONT OF PORCH AND STOOP

SECTION CD

DOOR SILL

SCALE ⅜ INCH TO THE FOOT

ANGLE BEAD "O"

ARCHITRAVE "N"

SCALE 1½ INCH TO THE FOOT.

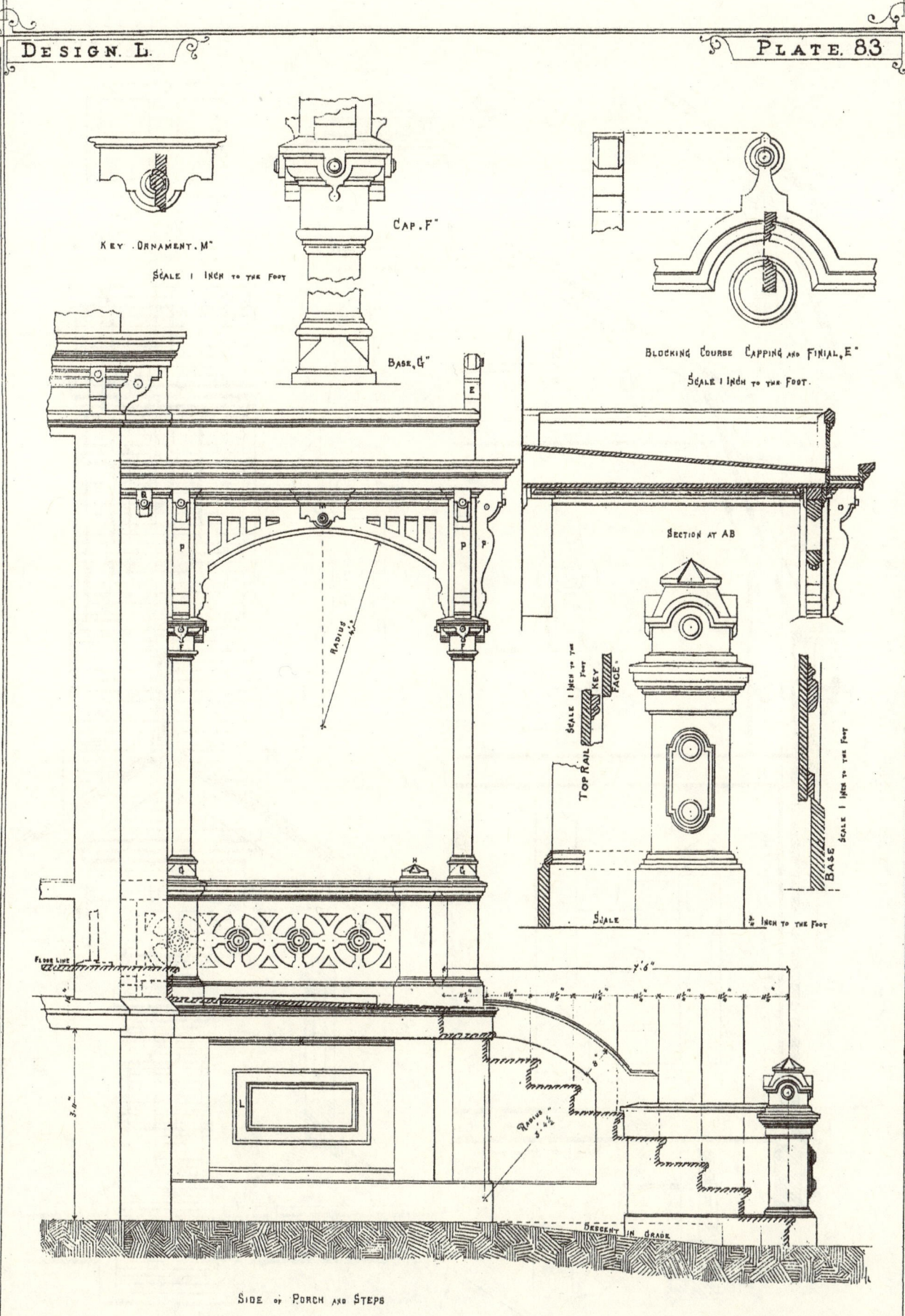

KEY .ORNAMENT. M"

SCALE 1 INCH TO THE FOOT

CAP. F"

BASE. G"

BLOCKING COURSE CAPPING AND FINIAL. E"

SCALE 1 INCH TO THE FOOT.

SECTION AT AB

RADIUS

TOP RAIL

KEY

FACE

SCALE 1 INCH TO THE FOOT

BASE SCALE 1 INCH TO THE FOOT

SCALE ⅜ INCH TO THE FOOT

FLOOR LINE

RADIUS 3' 4½"

DESCENT IN GRADE.

SIDE OF PORCH AND STEPS

SCALE ⅜ INCH TO THE FOOT.

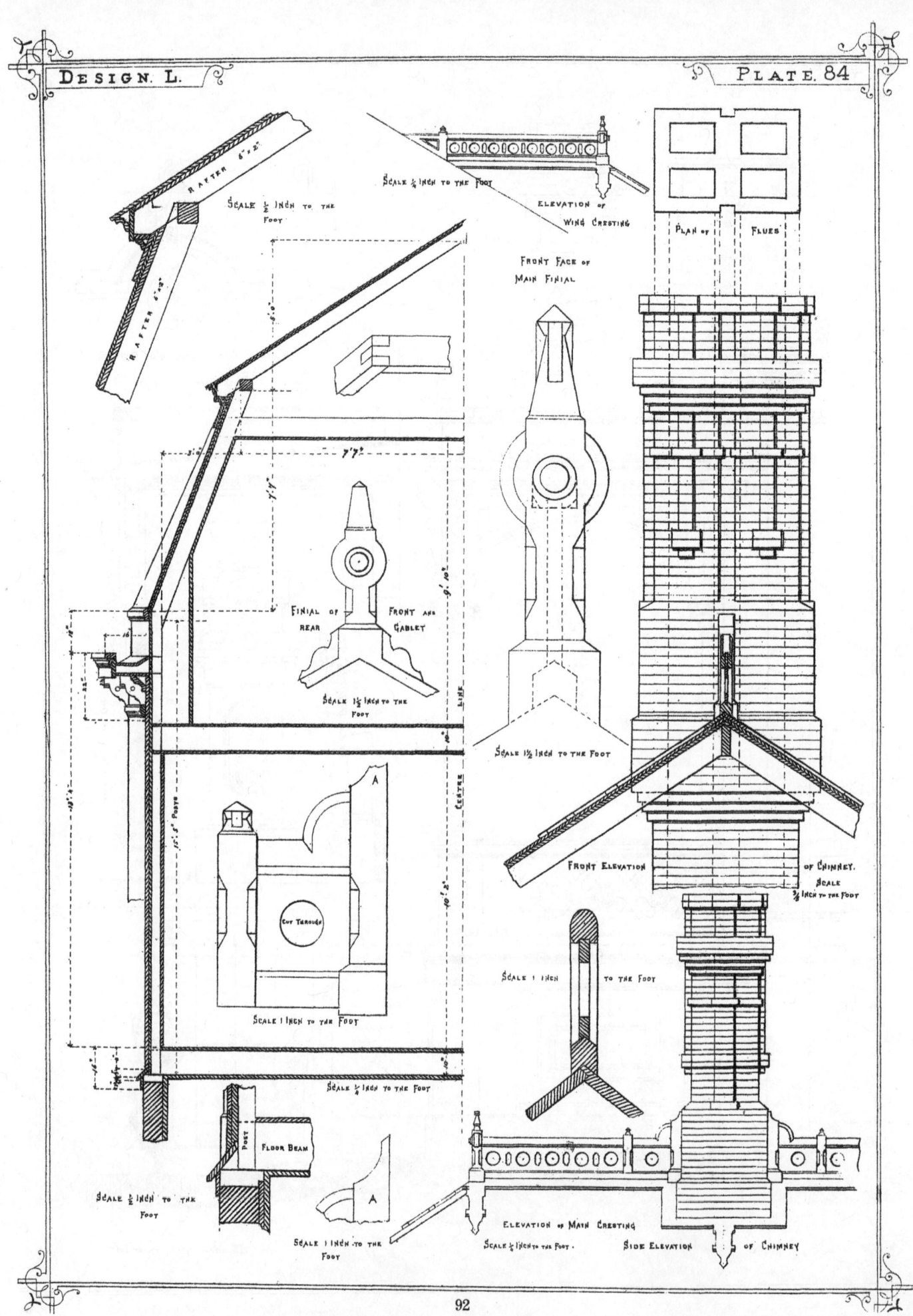

SCALE ½ INCH TO THE
FOOT

RAFTER 6"2"

RAFTER 6"2"

SCALE ¼ INCH TO THE FOOT

ELEVATION OF
WING CRESTING

PLAN OF   FLUES

FRONT FACE OF
MAIN FINIAL

FINIAL OF   FRONT AND
REAR   GABLET

SCALE 1½ INCH TO THE
FOOT

SCALE 1½ INCH TO THE FOOT

FRONT ELEVATION   OF CHIMNEY.
SCALE
¾ INCH TO THE FOOT

CUT THROUGH

A

SCALE 1 INCH TO THE FOOT

SCALE 1 INCH   TO THE FOOT

SCALE ¼ INCH TO THE FOOT

POST

FLOOR BEAM

SCALE ½ INCH TO THE
FOOT

A

SCALE 1 INCH TO THE
FOOT

SCALE ½ INCH TO THE FOOT.

ELEVATION OF MAIN CRESTING

SIDE ELEVATION   OF CHIMNEY

FRONT ELEVATION.

SCALE ⅛" = 1'

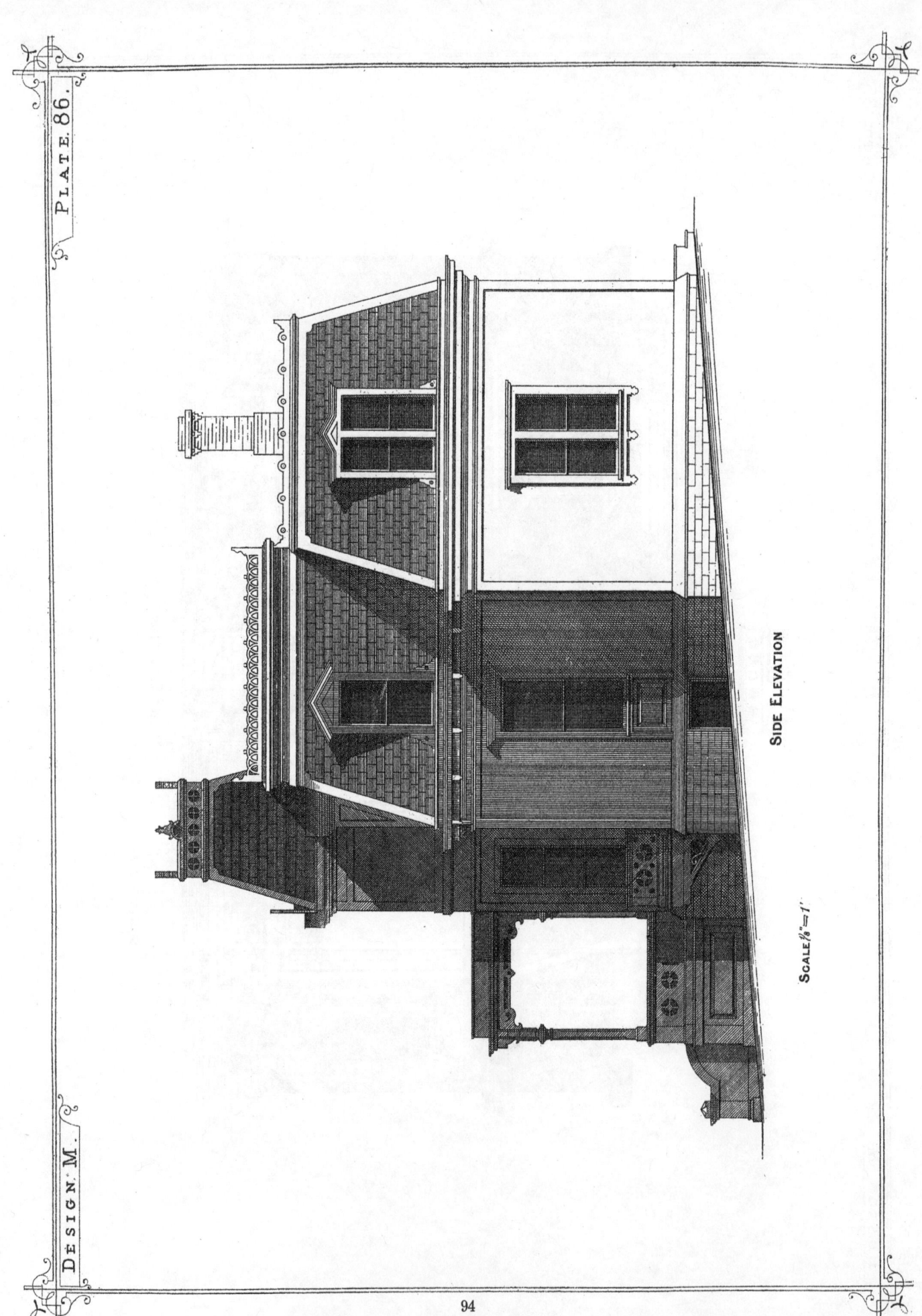

SIDE ELEVATION

SCALE ⅛"=1'

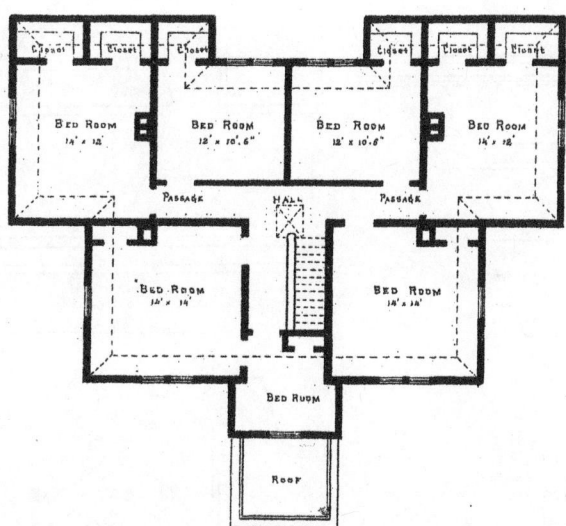

SECOND STORY PLAN.

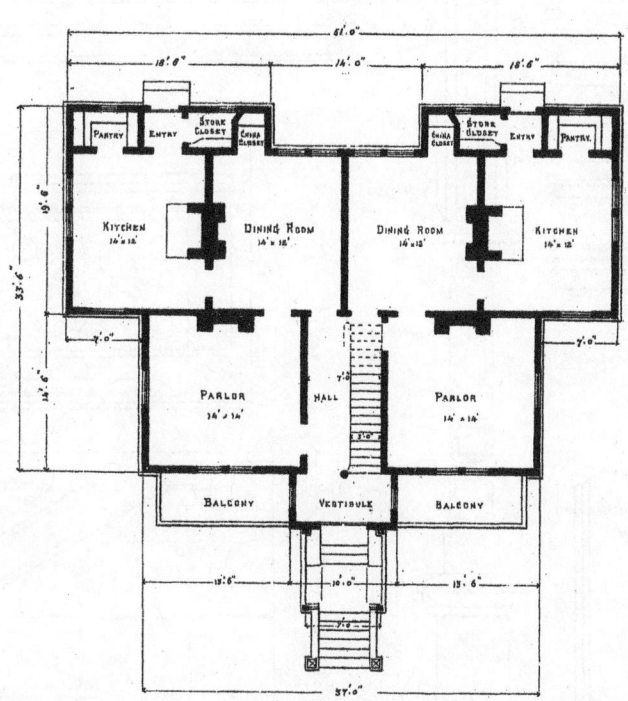

GROUND PLAN

SCALE ⅛ INCH TO THE FOOT

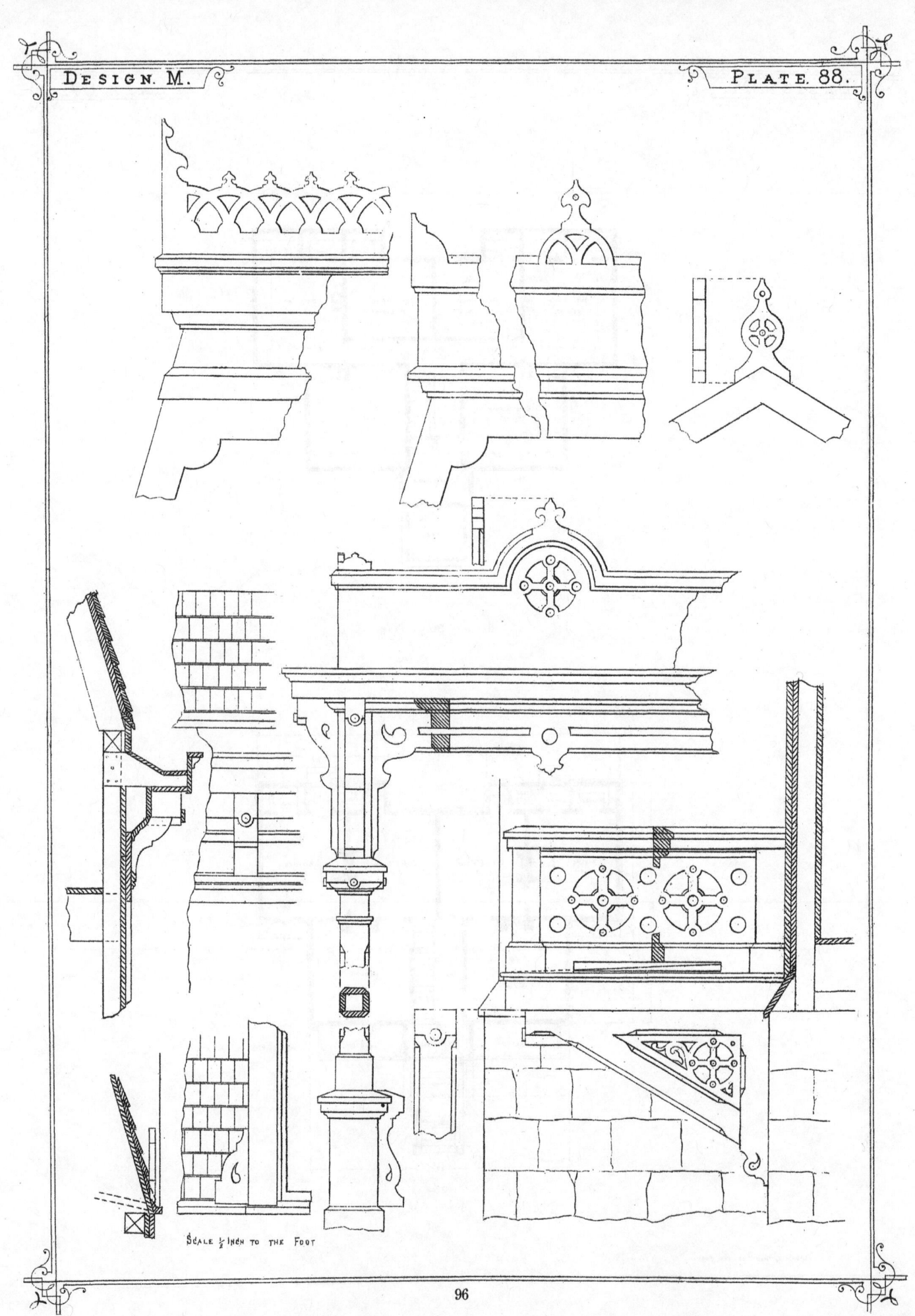

Scale ½ Inch to the Foot

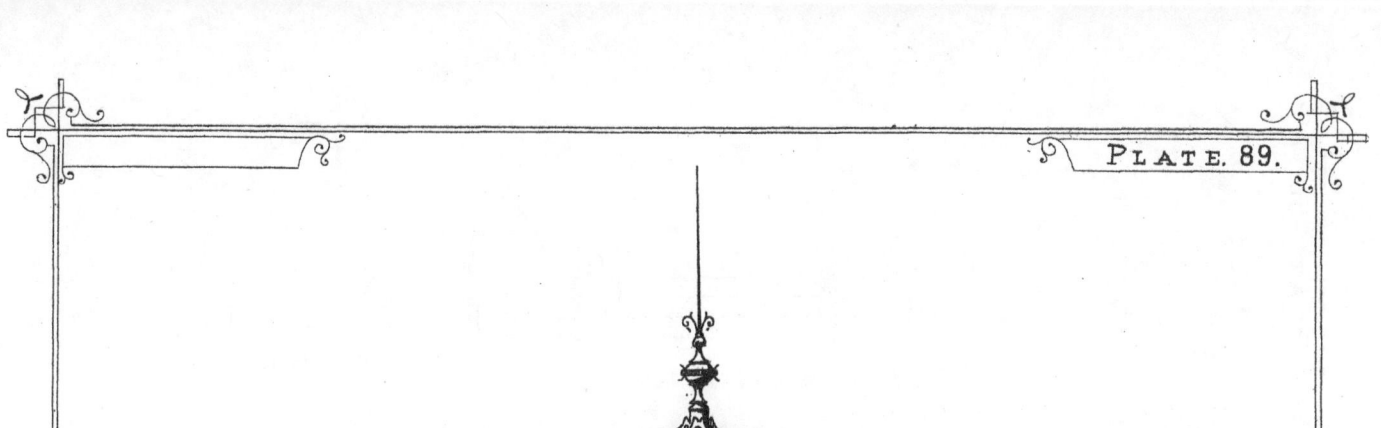

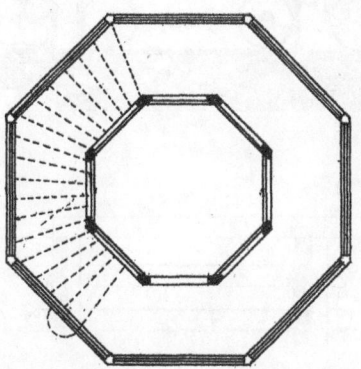

SUMMER HOUSE

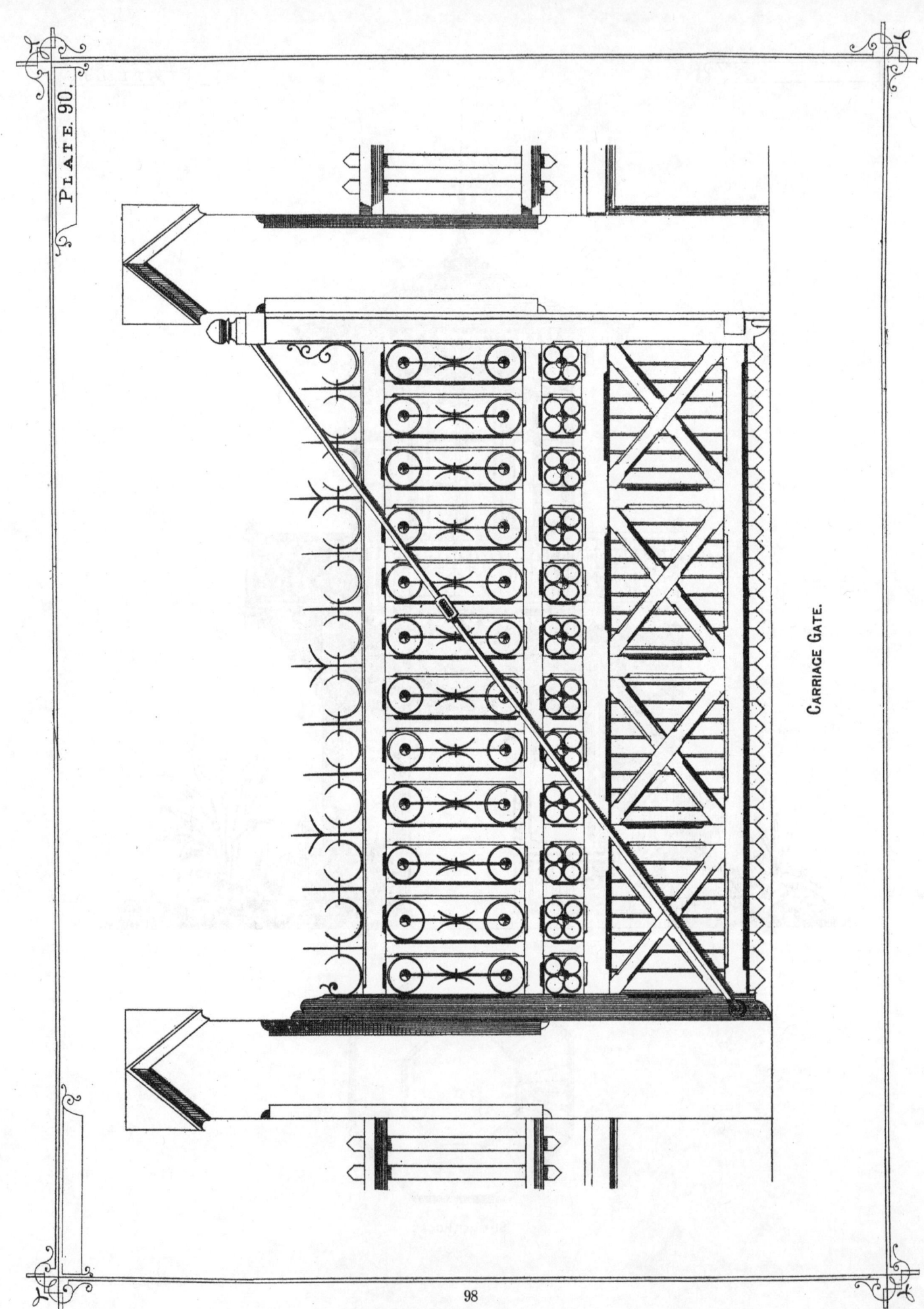

CARRIAGE GATE.

ORNAMENTAL GABLET

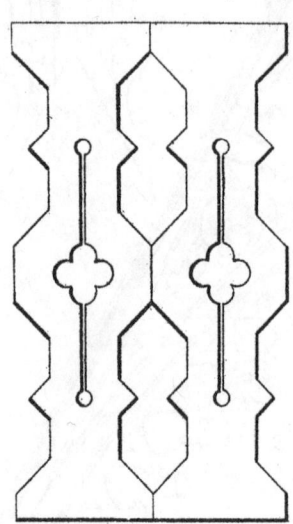
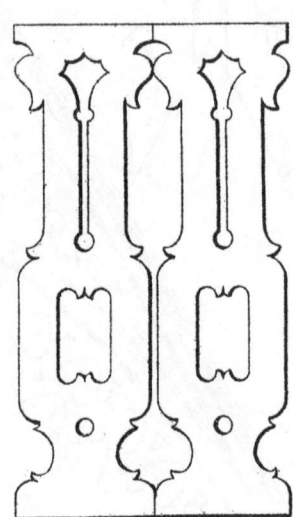

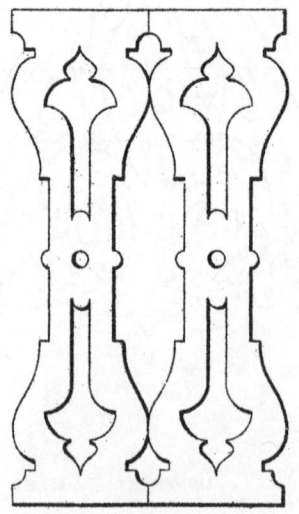
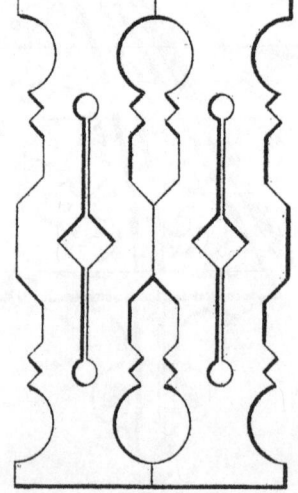

BALUSTRADES AND PANELS.

PORCH.

CRESTING FOR ROOFS

ORNAMENTAL GABLET FOR BARN.

VINE ARBOR.

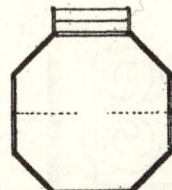

TOOL HOUSE

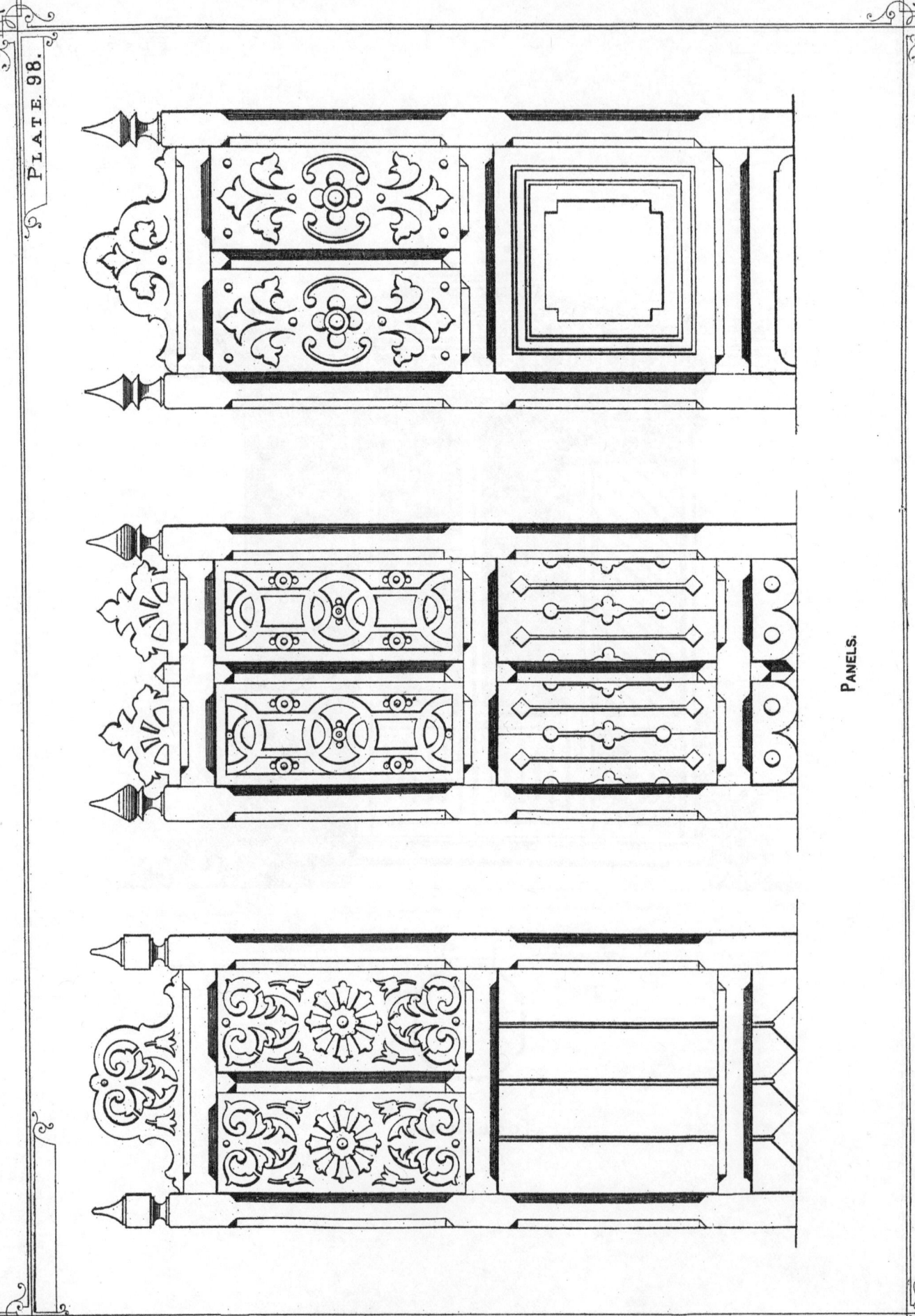

PANELS.

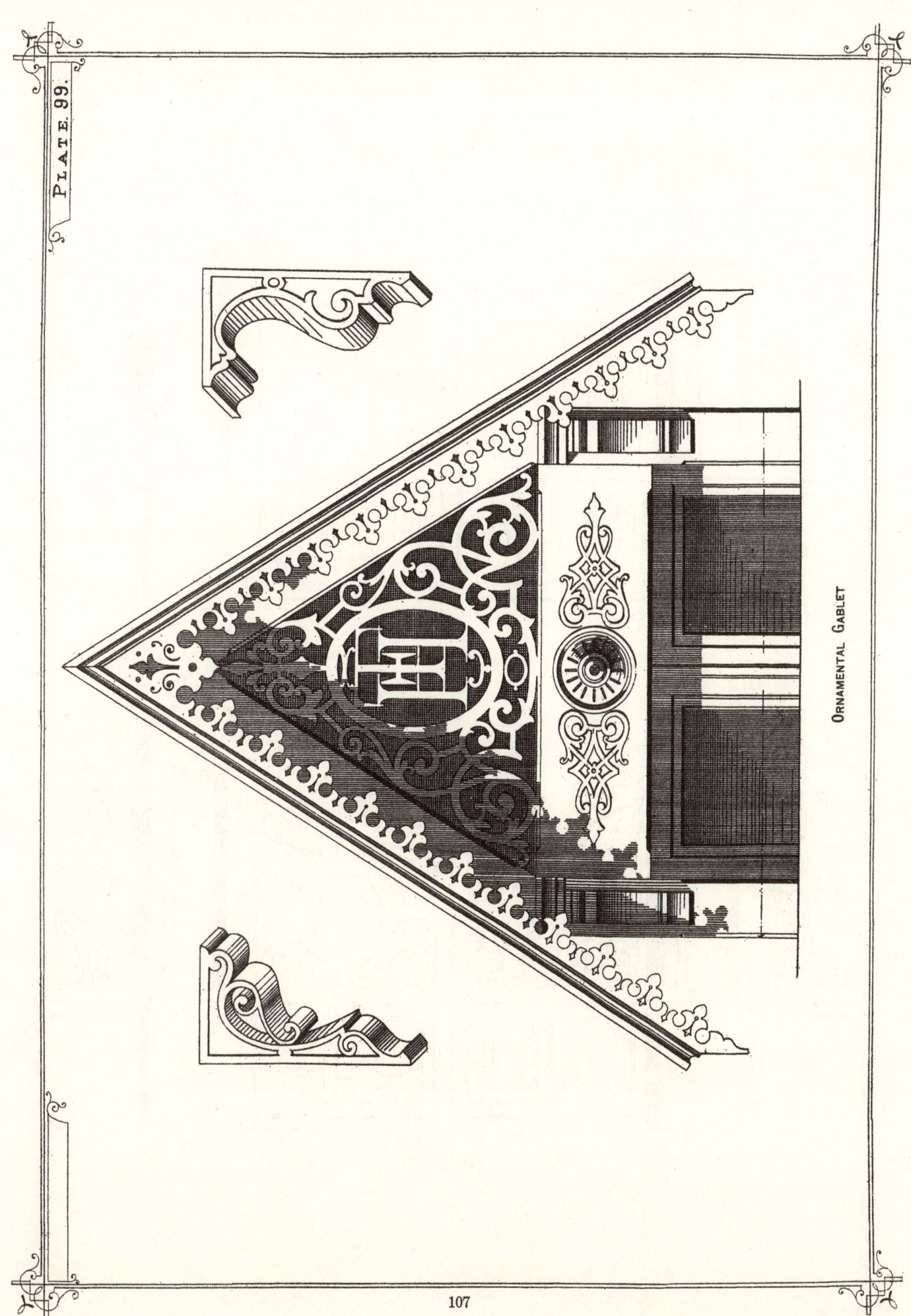

Ornamental Gablet

CARRIAGE GATE.

CARRIAGE GATE.